ZAHRA BATOOL

CW00920474

from one sister
to another, with love

leaf
publishing
house

With the hope to inspire generations of believing women
today, and those that are yet to come

bi idhnillah

DEDICATIONS

To every woman who is trying to better herself, and trying to connect with her Creator and her faith.

This book is for you.

INTRODUCTION

In the name of Allah, the Entirely Merciful, the Especially Merciful.

Women are a most important, integral part of society, and hold immense value in Islam. Many a book has been written informing women of their duties. These books are very important, and I pray Allah rewards the authors and scholars who have done so.

However, I feel that some of these books are often written by men, and can sometimes be talking at women, rather than talking to women.

I wanted to write a book that is not based around just telling women what they must do, or not do to be considered good women, but rather to encourage those who are reading it as I can relate to the different struggles that many sisters are facing today.

There is a general lack of understanding of the Deen, and as we live in a time in which knowledge is so easily accessible, many an issue is contorted and misunderstood due to independent learning without scholarly guidance.

I am hoping this book can be a message of hope above all else, and a means of clarity and encouragement. I have included a few topics that may seem random at first, but I feel they are very important for us to focus on as women.

This is not written at you my dear sister, but rather it is written for you. I pray it proves to be a source of comfort for you and a little reminder that you are loved by your Lord, and have much value in the Deen.

PART I

RIGHTEOUS WOMEN- RULINGS & RIGHTS

CHAPTER 1

INSPIRATIONAL MUSLIM WOMEN

Living the life of a Muslimah (muslim woman), in the 21st century is not easy at all. We have our highs and our lows, our struggles and our victories, and this is my attempt to remind you my dear sister, that you are valued, respected and loved more than you know.

Allah, Our Lord and Creator, has favoured us by making us amongst the believing women. It is our duty now to try and understand what that actually means, the purpose of our life, and what is required from us and why.

Muslim women are often stereotyped as being oppressed, uneducated and weak and I hope this book helps clear some common misunderstandings that are widespread about our status in Islam. It can be so overwhelmingly draining to be constantly exposed to and forcefully fed these negative narratives about ourselves and I firmly believe it is time we learn and fully recognise the potential and value we have when we embrace our Islamic identity wholeheartedly.

We are not weak and oppressed as the media often portrays us to be. We are powerful and intelligent and our belief gives us strength and purpose. Islam has given us respect and has uplifted our position in society. It is our pride, our identity and our moral compass in life.

Throughout history, women have sometimes had power and influence and in other times they have been stripped of all dignity and deemed to be the inferior gender.   Islam came at a time when the majority of women did not have any rights and in general were treated extremely poorly and abused. In Arabia for example a widespread custom at the time was for girls to be be buried alive by their fathers simply for being born female.

However, even in these dark times there were women of noble status who were respected by all, one of them being Khadija bint Khuwaylid, the first wife of our Prophet Muhammad ﷺ.

The arrival of Islam transformed the society with laws that honoured the rights of everyone.

Women were honoured and had a valued place in society; some becoming warriors, scholars, nurses, business women and others great mothers and God fearing home makers.

In Islam we have been given so many brilliant women to aspire to be like, and so many role models to learn from and try to emulate. We should know their names and we should know a little about them.

Sometimes we admire certain role models but we struggle to be like them without changing ourselves drastically, because the role models we have chosen are so different to our individual personalities.

Islam does not ask us to change who we are; it just asks us to be the best version of ourselves that we can be. Nor are we expected to all be exactly the same, perfect and free from all sins. We are human and so are flawed. But what is expected from us is to recognise our faults, pray for forgiveness, and always try to be better.

We were not created the same. Our individuality is what makes us so special. We are blessed! For Allah ﷻ has granted us so many women who we can look up to throughout our history. Great women each with their own individual personalities and quirks, and I promise you, you will find one whose character and personality is much like yours, and so it will be easy to emulate her, God Willing.

It is very important to know about these Muslimaat (believing women), for the more we know about them and learn about them, the more we naturally desire to be like them. They were the first believing women who excelled in their faith, and their lives are beautiful examples for us.

These women were special. They were fearless in the face of oppression, fought against tyranny and endured much hardship for the sake of Islam. Their blood was spilt, their wealth was spent, and they gave birth to the generations of pious men and women who came after them. These blessed ladies understood that this life is not worth hoarding, or competing over. They lived for a higher purpose than competing on trivial things such as who has better clothing or food. They used their life in the Dunya (world) to work towards the Hereafter. That is really the true purpose of all of our lives.

My beloved sister, you also are a woman of substance. You are a woman searching for the pleasure of Allah and for that reason I congratulate you.

For Allah ﷻ says in the Holy Qur'an,

And those who strive for Us - We will surely guide them to Our ways. And indeed, Allah is with the doers of good.

(Surah al 'Ankabut, verse 69)

Let's do a simple exercise together. Close your eyes and try to name all the wives of the Prophets, and the Sahabiyat (female companions) that you know.

Now close your eyes and name all the celebrities you know.

Do you know more names of the former or of the latter? If you know more celebrity names, then let's change that and try to learn more names of the pious women from our history, in sha Allah

These are ladies who excelled in their faith and brought benefit to their communities. Women who worked hard and deserve to be recognised and known.

Names of a few prominent women in Islam

Maryam- daughter of Imran

The blessed mother of Isa alayhi slaam. The pious woman after whom a whole Surah has been named in the Holy Qur'an. One of the best of women in Paradise.

She grew up sheltered and cared for in the house of Allah ﷻ, by Prophet Zakariyya alayhi slaam and even he was surprised to see that she was provided with special rizq (food and sustenance) from Allah ﷻ. This shows her beautiful status in the sight of The Creator ﷻ.

She was extremely pious and her modesty was unmatched. She was one of the only women in her time to be chosen for devout worship, as it was commonplace for only men to be chosen for this at that time. She was rewarded with a miraculous pregnancy and a miraculous birth, as she gave birth to Isa alayhi slaam without a man having ever touched her. She placed her entire trust in Allah ﷻ and we learn so much from her attitude in life.

Women are told the good news of their pregnancy by a doctor, midwife or even a pregnancy test, but how lofty was her status, that she was given the glad tidings by Allah ﷻ!

Lets for a minute just imagine how scared and worried she must have been about the reaction of her people when she, a pious unmarried woman, would return to them with a baby in her arms. However, she never doubted that Allah's help is near and she trusted that He would ease all of her affairs. Her immense tawakkul (reliance upon Allah) gave her strength and courage and made her amongst the most beloved to Allah.

Allah ﷻ says in the Holy Quran,

"O Mary, indeed Allah has chosen you and purified you and chosen you above the women of the worlds."

(Surah Ali'-Imran verse 42)

From her story we learn that if we obey Allah, no matter what befalls us, we will always be Protected by Him.

She was a single mother who birthed and raised one of the most well known and loved Prophets of Allah. People mocked her and shamed her and called her unchaste and she bore it patiently. As a result Allah honoured her with such a stamp of piety that He Himself praises her in the Holy Qur'an,

And [the example of] Mary, the daughter of 'Imran, who guarded her chastity, so We blew into [her garment] through Our angel, and she believed in the words of her Lord and His scriptures and was of the devoutly obedient.

(Surah At Tahrim, verse 12)

Hajar, mother of Isma'il alayhi slaam

The revered wife of Ibrahim alayhi slaam. A strong, brave woman, who is known for her sacrifices, determination, patience and submission to the will of Allah.

Allah ﷻ loved her action of running up and down the mounts of Safa and Marwah so much, that he made it obligatory upon all muslims to follow in her footsteps during Hajj and Umrah. It's worth mentioning that it is men who have to run as she did in her footsteps, and women are just to walk briskly.

She is the wife of a Prophet and the mother of a Prophet, peace be upon them. What a beautiful honour. In all of her affairs, she bowed her head in submission and accepted the Will of Allah ﷻ without complaining, and kept firm faith that it was all Allah's plan. Indeed Allah's plan is the best of plans.

Allah ﷻ told Ibrahim alayhi slaam to leave her in the middle of the desert with her baby Isma'il alayhi slaam and he did. Any woman would be heartbroken and distraught and feel betrayed in this situation. But she knew it was the will of her Lord, and knew it meant that He ﷻ had a plan for her and her son; so she accepted it with her whole heart and did not complain.

To be left all alone, in the middle of the hot arabian desert, with no water, no people, no community in sight, must have been a very scary prospect for her. And with her provisions running out, even more worrying. However she knew Allah ﷻ would provide for her and that satisfied her. She had nothing but love and respect for her husband who she understood was doing as Allah ﷻ had commanded him to do. Her patience kept her steadfast and her faith in Allah protected her from any doubts.

May Allah be pleased with her.

From how she handled this episode in her life, we can understand just how strong and resilient she was.

She protected and nurtured her son Isma'il alayhi slaam in the wilderness and for the most part raised him alone.

As she ran back and forth, up and down the mounts of Safa and Marwa in search of water for her thirsty babe, Allah, from His Mercy caused water to appear from the ground under her son's feet and till today thousands upon thousands of believers drink their fill of this blessed water of ZamZam.

ZamZam water has been given this name due to Hajar repeatedly saying "Zam Zam" (stop flowing) as she feared the spring may dry up if it flowed continuously.

Travellers came in search of water and she gave them permission to settle. In turn, communities formed and Makkah became a bustling city of trade and relief for pilgrims.

Allah has raised Hajar's station and made her life a lesson for the believers. Her story is embedded in our history and so her example lives on as a reminder for us all.

There may be a time when you go through a hardship where you feel alone- remember her and take comfort from her example and turn to Allah as she did.

Aasiyah, wife of Pharoah

Second mother to Musa alayhi slaam as she raised him as her own. Allah ﷻ had placed affection and mercy in her heart. She accepted the message of Musa and Harun, (peace and blessings be upon them both) and became a firm believer despite being married to the oppressive Pharoah who called himself God.

She was persecuted and beaten for her faith and yet she stayed strong and her Imaan (faith) never wavered. Pharoah upon learning about her belief in Allah, did all he could to try and degrade and humiliate her.

She was married to the most oppressive tyrant of the time, and yet she was not judged because of her relationship to him, rather she was honoured because of her own deeds and faith. This is the Supreme Justice of Allah ﷻ; He Who Judges all according to their own deeds.

Allah ﷻ says in the Holy Qur'an:

"And Allah presents an example of those who believed: the wife of Pharaoh, when she said, "My Lord, build for me near You a house in Paradise and save me from

Pharaoh and his deeds and save me from the wrongdoing people."

(Surah At-Tahrim, verse 11)

From her du'a we learn she wanted nothing more than to be close to Allah and to her, that was all that mattered. Not the pain, not the suffering or humiliation that she was enduring. She requested nothing but to be near her Lord.

She was a Queen, and had all the wealth and comforts this world has to offer. She easily could have kept her faith hidden and enjoyed the pleasures of the world but she chose not to sacrifice her faith for the sake of worldly pleasures and ease.

She had servants and rubies and riches, yet she was willing to give up all her comforts and her life for the sake of the Deen. In turn Aasiyah was given the glad tidings of Paradise and is revered as one of the leading women in Jannah.

The Prophet ﷺ said:

"Sufficient for you among the women of mankind are Mariam bint 'Imran, Khadijah bint Khuwailid, Faatimah bint Muhammad and Aasiyah the wife of Fir'awn."

(Jami At Tirmidhi)

Pharoah eventually had her killed because she refused to renounce her belief in Allah ﷻ. He did all he could to degrade her, yet her name and praise lives on. Allah showed her, her abode in the Hereafter before she died and so she passed away laughing in joy at what she had seen. Aasiyah will forever be an example of a woman who chose the Hereafter over all the glitters and comforts of this world, and whose love for Allah made her challenge her own husband, despite being well aware of all the many horrific ways he could torment and torture her. Her strength and status will always be remembered and she is known as one of the greatest women who have walked this Earth.

Names of the wives of the Prophet ﷺ

1. Khadija
2. Sawdah
3. A'isha
4. Hafsah bint Umar
5. Zaynab bint Khuzaimah
6. Umm Salamah
7. Zaynab bint Jahsh
8. Juwairiah bint al harith
9. Umm Habiba
10. Saffiyah
11. Maymunah

May Allah be pleased with them all.

Khadija- Daughter of Khwaylid

One of the most noble women of her time and the first wife of the last and final Prophet, Muhammad ﷺ. First believer and supporter of the cause of Islam. She was a successful business woman who sacrificed all her wealth and her worldly comforts in the way of the Deen, and to comfort the Messenger of Allah ﷺ. She was known as Tahirah (the pure one) prior to Islam, in an age in which purity was scarce. She had been widowed twice prior to her marriage to the beloved of Allah ﷺ, and she was respected amongst the old and the young in and around Makkah.

She comforted the Messenger of Allah ﷺ and gave him hope

when others turned him away. He ﷺ in turn gave her the glad tidings of a palace in paradise, free from noise and from fatigue.

The Prophet ﷺ said,

"The best of the world's women is Mary (in her lifetime), and the best of the world's women is Khadija (in her lifetime).

(Sahih al Bukhari)

The Prophet ﷺ, never married another woman during her life and he loved her deeply. It was the custom of the time to wed more than one woman, but it was telling of their love and special bond that they had a monogamous marriage for 25 years till she passed away.

She was the mother to all of his children, except one, and she cared for him and believed in him when others did not. She never doubted him and gave him the confidence and courage he needed in the early days of Islam and continued to do so till she passed away.

She is a shining example of how to be a loving wife, and mother and a firm believer.

Khadija was a wise woman and upheld her duties beautifully. Years after her passing he ﷺ still wept in memory of her.

He ﷺ once said about Khadija radi allaha anha, in reply to something A'isha had said,

"Her love had been nurtured in my heart by Allah Himself."

(Sahih Muslim)

Allah had blessed her with riches of the world, however this did not make her proud or haughty. Rather she was renowned for distributing wealth amongst the poor and needy, financially assisting her relatives and friends and providing women in her community with dowries for their marriages.

This woman is the great woman in whose lap Islam flourished and in whose reassuring words and comforting arms the Prophet ﷺ found peace, after he disclosed his fears of the responsibility which had been placed upon him by Allah.

Her overwhelming trust in him is clear from her famous response,

"Allah will never disgrace you, while you are kind and considerate to your relations, help the poor and the forlorn and bear their burdens? You treat guests with honour and help those who are in distress."

Just in these words alone, her love, belief and respect for her husband is clear to see.

Her services for the Deen were described by The Messenger of Allah ﷺ when he said:

"She believed in me when no one else did; she accepted Islam when people rejected me; and she helped and comforted me when there was no one else to lend me a helping hand."

(Musnad Imam Ahmad Ibn Hanbal)

She was honoured with greetings sent to her by Allah, honoured with the glad tidings of her final abode in Paradise and was honoured with the opportunity to serve and aid the Messenger of Allah with her love, her valuable advice and with her wealth.

May Allah be pleased with her.

Sawdah- Daughter of Zam'ah

After Khadija radi Allaha anha passed away, the Messenger of Allah ﷺ was left to raise a small family and so he married Sawdah radi Allaha anha. She was a widow and was amongst the first believers who migrated to Abyssinia. She had small children herself with no one to care for them and so the Messenger of Allah married her as her situation was similar to his own. Thus they were able to care for each other and for their children.

She had the great privilege of being married to the beloved of Allah ﷺ for three years before he took another wife, and she also had the honour of being amongst those few believers who were rewarded with two migrations.

She was also one of the early converts to Islam.

Sawdah radi Allaha anha was known for being a very kind, generous and gentle woman, and she gave often in charity. She had a particular fondness for A'isha radi Allaha anha and even gifted her her 'day' that she had with the Messenger of Allah ﷺ.

A'isha reported:

"Never did I find a woman more loving to me than Sawdah bint Zam'a. I wished I could be exactly like her who was passionate. As she became old, she had gifted over her day (which she had) with Allah's Messenger ﷺ, to A'isha. She said: "I have given over my day with you to A'isha." So Allah's Messenger ﷺ alloted two days to A'isha, her own day (when it was her turn) and that of Sawdah.

(Sahih Muslim)

Both women had a bond and shared a similar sense of humour. They often laughed and teased each other and always were very tolerant of each other, despite their age gap.

There is one story mentioned in ahadith of how A'isha and Sawdah (May Allah be pleased with them both) were sitting with the Messenger of Allah ﷺ. A'isha had made some food and told Sawdah to try some of it but she politely refused. Scooping some up in her hand A'isha playfully threatened to wipe it on her face if she did not try it. Sawdah still refused and so A'isha did exactly that.

Sawdah had her face covered in food. The Messenger of Allah ﷺ was laughing beside them, and he held the meal out and told Sawdah to take a handful and do the same to A'isha.

This shows how patient and good hearted Sawdah was. She understood it to be a joke and didn't lose her temper with A'isha. Despite her age she always joined in with pleasant pranks and games, showing she had a playful side to her.

Sawdah shared an affection based around sisterhood with all her co-wives and her piety and fear of Allah formed solid foundations of trust and respect.

A'isha- Daughter of Abu Bakr

She was one of the Ummahatul mu'mineen (mothers of the believers), a title given to the wives of the last and final Prophet, Muhammad ﷺ. She was very wise, beautiful and extremely beloved to the Messenger of Allah, and was the daughter of the great companion Abu Bakr radi allahu anhu.

Her chastity has been proven by Allah ﷺ in the Holy Qur'an and a great deal of knowledge that we have today about how our beloved Prophet ﷺ lived and behaved, was first remembered and then taught to others by A'isha Radiallaha anha.

She was one of the greatest scholars amongst women and men, and her acute memory has allowed over 2000 narrations to be preserved and passed down till they've reached us today. We know much about the Prophet's day to day life due to her. She was a source of knowledge and wisdom for both men and women and people travelled from far and wide to learn and soak up her flow of knowledge. She was one of the main contributors to the developing and interpretation of the Holy Qur'an and the knowledge of ahadith.

She was full of life, well versed in poetry and had knowledge of medicine and Islamic jurisprudence. She was outspoken, intelligent and had strong opinions, yet at the same time she was humble and righteous. She is a beautiful role model for Muslim women, young and old alike, and her example encourages sisters to seek knowledge and have a scholarly approach to life.

The Prophet ﷺ loved her dearly and he passed away in her home whilst his head was resting in her lap.

Some of the greatest companions, such as Umar ibn al Khattab radi allahu anhu came to her for advice and scholars benefited and are still benefiting from her vast knowledge.

The Messenger of Allah peace be upon him said:

"The virtue of 'A'isha over women is like the virtue of Tharid over all other foods."

(Jami at-Tirmidhi)

Her narrations have given profound insight on how the relationship between a man and his wife should be, from experience and lessons that she learnt through her own relationship with the Messenger of Allah ﷺ.

She was a generous woman who distributed any and all wealth that was gifted to her and she lived a life of taqwa (God consciousness) and piety till the day she passed away. Having no children of her own, she took orphaned children in to her care and educated and provided for them.

In this is a lesson to all those sisters who despair and struggle with infertility, and also to those who shame women and look down upon them for not bearing children. Many sisters are struggling with this as the mental and emotional burdens brought on by the hurtful comments of others can be very difficult to bear.

It's important to note that some of the wives of the Messenger of Allah bore no children of their own. This did not take away from the amazing women they were and they contributed so much to the community and to Islam, which if they did have children, they may not have been able to do, and Allah knows best. They are from the best women in the Dunya and the Aakhirah.

She was not afraid to stand up for her faith and her ideals, and she participated in many Battles, in which her leadership and courage showed that women have a voice to be heard in Islam and a right to be involved and have some authority in male-dominated activities.

Our mother A'isha was the wife of the beloved Messenger ﷺ in this life and in the next and we pray we can walk in her footsteps, taking benefit from the many words of wisdom she has left us.

Hafsah- Daughter of Umar

The daughter of Umar radi Allahu anhu, the great companion, khalifa and friend of the Prophet Muhammad ﷺ. She grew up amongst senior companions of the Messenger of Allah ﷺ and embodied their characteristics. She was a devout worshipper and would often fast during the day and spend her night praying Tahajjud (voluntary night prayer).

She had been married to a man called Khunais, but was widowed whilst she was still young, after which she had the great honour of being married to the Messenger of Allah ﷺ.

Hafsah was a very well educated woman. She could read and write which was extremely uncommon even amongst the men in those times.

She was a hafidha (woman who has memorised the entire Holy Qur'an) and was also a narrator of 60 ahadith describing the actions and habits of the Prophet Muhammad ﷺ. Her knowledge of religious matters was very sound and she had a strong thirst to learn.

She had an inquisitive nature and often asked questions when she desired clarity on a matter. This enhanced her intellect and helped her comprehend the intricacies of Quranic injunctions more deeply.

The Messenger of Allah ﷺ, gave her the responsibility of safe-keeping the parchments on which the Holy Qur'an was inscribed. After his passing, and when many of the hufaadh (people who have memorised the Qur'an) were killed in the battle of Yamama, it became necessary to have the Qur'an compiled in book form. She was consulted on this matter and she had the unique honour of guarding the first compiled, written Holy Qur'an, which she preserved and looked after until Uthman radi Allahu anhu became the next khalifa; it was then passed on to him.

She passed away in the month of Shaban, and was buried in Jannat-ul-Baqi alongside her blessed co-wives.

We should take her thirst for knowledge as a push to memorise the Qur'an and study our Deen.

Zaynab- Daughter of Khuzaimah

Very little is known about Zaynab bint Khuzaimah, and this may be due to the fact that she passed away in Madinah very soon after her marriage to the Messenger of Allah ﷺ.

What is known is that she had a heart of gold and was extremely generous and looked after the poor and needy so much so, that she was given the title "Umm-ul-Masakeen", (Mother of the poor) due to her charity work and compassion towards those in need.

Generosity is always rewarded by Allah, in this life and in the Hereafter. We should follow in her footsteps and give with a generous hand to those in need.

Her husband had been killed in battle and her marriage to the Messenger of Allah ﷺ set an example for others and it became praiseworthy to marry the widows that martyrs left behind, providing them security in this manner.

Widowed women find it very difficult to marry in many societies today, however this is contrary to the examples we have from the example of the Prophet ﷺ and of his companions. They rushed to marry widows and helped care for and protect them and their children.

Umme Salamah

One of the wives of the Prophet Muhammad ﷺ. Previously she had been married to Abu Salamah who was one of the righteous Sahaba (companions of the Messenger of Allah). He passed away due to an injury he had received during the battle of Uhud.

She was a passionate, pious and firm believer and loved Abu Salamah dearly as he had been a kind, gentle husband and they both had been through so much together. They were from the few companions who migrated to Abyssinia, due to the increased persecution at the hands of the Quraish, and were amongst the first companions who accepted Islam. When the Messenger of Allah ﷺ gave permission to the sahaba (companions) to emigrate to Madinah, they were among the first to leave.

Upon seeing her leave, her tribe forcefully separated her from her son and her husband for over a year. She wept bitterly every night until she was reunited with them both.

Sometime later in her life, after Abu Salamah's death she received proposals from prominent Sahaba including the likes of Abu Bakr, but she turned them all down because she felt none were better for her than Abu Salamah.

Lastly she was offered marriage by the Messenger of Allah ﷺ and she accepted, for who could be better than the beloved of Allah!

Umme Salamah reported Allah's Messenger ﷺ as saying:

"Whenever you visit the sick or the dead, supplicate for good because angels say "Ameen" to whatever you say."

She added: When Abu Salamah died, I went to the Messenger of Allah and said: O Messenger of Allah ﷺ, Abu Salamah has died. He told me to recite:

"O Allah, forgive me and him (Abu Salamah) and give me a better substitute than he."

So I said (this) and Allah gave me in exchange Muhammad, who is better for me than Abu Salamah."

(Sahih Muslim)

The fact that so many of the sahaba and even the Prophet ﷺ requested her hand in marriage, shows just how virtuous and honourable of a woman she was. This also shows that a widowed woman should have no problems in finding a spouse. Unfortunately in many societies widows face difficulty in marrying again. This attitude was not found in the time of the Messenger of Allah and widowed and divorced women were approached for marriage often.

With all her virtues, Umme Salamah also had a deep understanding of the Deen, was an expert in jurisprudence, and was the reliable narrator of many ahadith. The Messenger of Allah ﷺ would discuss different matters with her and he valued her advice greatly.

She showed great leadership skills at Hudaibiya when she told the Prophet ﷺ to shave his head and offer sacrifice, as that way the sahabah will follow him. This is a great example of her wisdom and ability to take lead and give correct advice when needed. With her loving and caring manner she had advised the Messenger of Allah ﷺ and he had acted upon her advice. In turn the sahaba started shaving and cutting their hair too without The Prophet ﷺ having to repeat himself again. This pleased the Messenger of Allah ﷺ and he smiled so much so that his molar teeth were visible.

She had used her caring manner and intellect to diffuse the situation and solve the problem at hand, and she has been unanimously praised for this in all the narrations which mention this incident.

We can take many lessons from her example. Using the intellect and naturally caring nature Allah has granted us, we can also be a source of peace and joy for our loved ones.

If we take from Umme Salamah's character and listen to and advise our loved ones correctly, we can be a source of comfort and add value to our relationships.

Zaynab- Daughter of Jahsh

Zaynab was of noble lineage from the tribe of Quraish and was brought up in luxury and riches. She was the cousin of the Messenger of Allah ﷺ and was known to be beautiful as well as being from the upper class of society.

Her original birth name was Barra (meaning very pious) and

the Messenger of Allah ﷺ changed her name to Zaynab, as self praise is disliked in Islam.

She had been married to the adopted son and freed slave of the Messenger of Allah ﷺ, Zayd ibn Haritha. However, due to the difference in their backgrounds they didn't get along and clashed often. When their marriage became unhappy and unbearable, and there was no hope of reconciliation, RasulAllah ﷺ allowed them to divorce.

After her divorce from Zayd, she was married to the Messenger of Allah ﷺ.

Their marriage was backed by verses of the Holy Qur'an and demonstrated that in Islam the adopted son is different to the natural son and their relevant rulings are different; hence it was permitted to marry a woman that was divorced by your adoptive son.

Zaynab was very proud of this fact and often said to her co-wives,

"Your families arranged your marriages but Allah ﷺ arranged my marriage from above the seven heavens."

The wives of the Messenger ﷺ were divided into two camps. A'isha and Hafsah were on one side and Zaynab and Umm Salamah were on the other side, and each side had friendly competition with the other.

A'isha radi Allaha anha, despite their rivalry, stated a very beautiful description of Zaynab, and praised her on more than one occasion. She said;

"And I never saw any woman who was better, more generous in giving charity, more keen to uphold the ties of kinship, and more generous in giving of herself in everything by means of which she could draw closer to Allah, than Zainab.

But she had a quick temper; however, she was also quick to calm down."

(Sunan An-Nasa'l)

Zaynab also spoke well of A'isha and when asked, she said she knew and she had seen nothing but good from her. At the time when A'isha was being slandered, she was one of the few who spoke in her favour. A'isha herself mentions this and says that Zaynab's piety and truthfulness is what saved her from speculation.

We can learn much from the way they differed with each other. They loved and respected each other despite their evident differences. They defended each other when needed and always spoke the truth.

Zaynab was known for her piety, her steadfastness upon the Deen of Allah, and for her truthfulness. She confined herself to her home after the passing of the Messenger of Allah ﷺ, and spent the rest of her days in teaching and worship.

She was the first of the wives of the Messenger of Allah ﷺ to pass away after his death.

Narrated by A'isha: Some of the wives of the Prophet ﷺ asked him, "Who amongst us will be the first to follow you (i.e. die after you)?" He ﷺ said, "Whoever has the longest hand."

So they started measuring their hands with a stick and Sawdah's hand turned out to be the longest. (When Zaynab bint Jahsh died first in the caliphate of Umar), we came to know that the long hand was a symbol of practising charity, so she was the first to follow the Prophet and she used to love to practice charity. (Sawdah died later in the caliphate of Mu'awiyah)

(Sahih al Bukhari)

Her exemplary piety and truthfulness makes her a beautiful role model for all sisters.

Juwairiah- Daughter of al Harith

Juwairiah was the daughter of the chief of the tribe of Banu Musta'liq. She was beautiful and had a level of beauty that was not common to see.

Prior to becoming muslim, she was captured in the battle that took place between the Muslims and her tribe. She was a strong woman who knew her place as a noble lady and so she went directly to the Messenger of Allah ﷺ asking to be freed.

The Messenger ﷺ not only agreed to free her but he also requested her hand in marriage and she accepted. In this way he honoured her whole tribe.

As a result the whole tribe accepted Islam, those of them who were captured were set free, and the war booty confiscated from them was given back to them with honour.

In praise of her, A'isha said that she knew no woman who brought more benefit to her people than Juwairiah.

She kept herself out of politics and busied herself in worship.

She was very young when she married the Messenger of Allah ﷺ and she was one of the last wives to pass away.

We only have a few ahadith narrated by her, one of which is my personal favourite; she records some words of supplication the Prophet ﷺ taught her.

It was narrated that Juwairiah bint al Harith said that:

The Prophet ﷺ passed by her while she was in the masjid supplicating, then he passed by her again when it was almost midday. He said to her: "Are you still here?"

She replied, "Yes." He said, "Shall I not teach you some words which you can say?

SubhanAllah adada khalqihi (x3) SubhanAllah rida nafsihi (x3) SubhanAllah zinata 'arshihi (x3) SubhanAllah midada Kalamatihi (x3)

(Glory be to Allah the number of His Creation (x3), Glory be to Allah as much as Pleases Him (x3), Glory be to Allah the weight of His Throne (x3), Glory be to Allah the number of His Words. (x3)

(Sunan An-Nasa'l)

Umm Habiba

Her name was Ramla bint Abi Sufyan, however she was more commonly known as Umm Habiba and this is how she is addressed in the books of ahadith.

She was the daughter of Abu Sufyaan, who was one of the leaders of Quraish and at that time an enemy of Islam. She however, accepted Islam and openly declared the shahada. This angered Abu Sufyaan and he tried to bring her back to the religion of their forefathers, however she stayed strong and firm upon the Deen and migrated with her husband Ubayd-Allah ibn Jahsh to Abyssinia. He passed away there suddenly, leaving her in a strange country with a young child. Upon hearing about her predicament, the Messenger of Allah ﷺ, sent her a marriage proposal and the King of Abyssinia, who had secretly accepted Islam, provided her Mahr and served as witness for the Nikkah.

She was a patient woman and Allah rewarded her patience by granting her the highest honour of being amongst the mothers of the believers.

She was blessed to see her father and brother accept Islam and this brought much joy to her as it was something she had desired for some time.

Umm Habiba was extremely pious, busying herself in worship and supplication and she also held the honour of being a narrator of ahadith.

She lived during many times of turmoil after the passing of the Messenger of Allah ﷺ, however she kept out of the politics and did not take a stance one way or the other.

She passed away during her brother Mu'awiyyah's rule and was buried amongst the other ummahatul mu'mineen who had passed away before her.

Saffiyah- Daughter of Huyayy

Saffiyah, was the daughter of a leader of the tribe of Banu Nadir. She was taken captive at the battle of Khaybar and with her permission the Messenger of Allah ﷺ married her, after which she accepted Islam. It is said that she could trace her lineage all the way back to Prophet Harun alayhi slaam.

She was soft hearted, of a quiet disposition and she faced all of her problems with considerable patience. The Messenger of Allah ﷺ defended her and provided her with honour and love when others mocked her, and comforted her with words of reassurance.

May Allah be pleased with her.

She was not welcomed by some of her co-wives and she felt the difficulties of being a new convert to the religion.

From what we know of her, she was known as a good cook and cooked often. She never showed arrogance and was always looking for ways to help others.

She is a great example of excellent character, patience and humility.

Maymunah

Maymunah was aunt to the great Sahabi and scholar of the Holy Qur'an, Ibn Abbas. He learnt much of his knowledge from her and she was known for being good hearted and jovial.

She was from a noble family from the tribe of Quraish.

She had been married twice prior to her marriage to the Messenger of Allah ﷺ. She had been divorced from her first husband and widowed by her second husband.

She sought the Messenger of Allah's hand in marriage herself and he ﷺ accepted. She wished to be wed to him with all her heart and she expressed this desire to her sister Umm al Fadhl, and she, in turn, spoke to her husband Al Abbas about it. He then went to the Messenger of Allah ﷺ and told him, and the Prophet ﷺ accepted the proposal. The wedding was held in a place called Saraf, which was roughly 10 miles from the city of Makkah.

This shows her love for the Prophet ﷺ and she was a woman who knew what she wanted and did what she could to get it.

Her name was also originally Barrah, but the Messenger of Allah ﷺ changed it to "Maymunah" (the blessed) in joy of the fact that her marriage with him marked his entrance and return into his hometown of Makkah after seven years.

Maymunah lived with the Prophet ﷺ for just over three years, until his death. She was good natured and got along well with all of her co-wives. There is no argument or even slight disagreement recorded in which she has a part.

She is a narrator of ahadith and was very knowledgeable.

Maymunah (May Allah be pleased with her) passed away in

51 AH. She was buried in Saraf in accordance with her will. She chose to be buried in the place that marked her marriage to the Messenger of Allah ﷺ, rather than to be buried in Jannat-ul-Baqi with the rest of her blessed co-wives.

May Allah be pleased with them all.

Names of the daughters of the Messenger of Allah ﷺ

1. Syeda Zainab
2. Syeda Ruqayyah
3. Syeda Umm Kulthoom
4. Syeda Fatimah

Faatimah- Daughter of Muhammad ﷺ

The youngest and most beloved daughter of the Prophet Muhammad ﷺ. Her modesty, piety and shyness were unmatched. She grew up in the purest of environments. Her mother Khadija, being the best of women and her father the best of all creation; the Messenger of Allah ﷺ. What a beautiful home to grow up in.

Faatimah herself was mother to Hassan and Hussain and wife to Ali, radi allahu anhum ajmaeen. What a blessed household. She was a strong, hard working woman, who spent her days and nights worshipping Allah ﷺ and looking after her family.

She had 4 prominent nicknames, Zahra, Batool, Umm al Hassan wal Husayn and Umm Abeeha.

Zahra, because of her beautiful complexion and because she was like a flower for her father.

Batool, because her piety and lack of desire for worldly possessions was described as matching Maryam alayhi slaams.

Umm al-Hassan wal-Hussain, for being the mother of her blessed sons; the dearest to the Messenger of Allah ﷺ and about whom He ﷺ said,

"Al-Hasan and Al-Husain are the chiefs of the youth of Paradise."

(Jami' At-Tirmidhi)

Umm Abeeha meaning "mother of her father", due to the love, care and protectiveness she felt and showed, towards the Messenger of Allah ﷺ, especially after the passing away of her mother. She was given the glad tidings of being the leader of the women in Paradise.

She walked like the Prophet ﷺ and talked like the Prophet ﷺ and resembled him the most, peace be upon them both.

The Messenger of Allah ﷺ used to rise for her when she would come to him, and greet her with much love and enthusiasm, and she would do the same. She lost her ability to smile after the passing away of the Messenger of Allah ﷺ out of grief and she passed away soon after.

She was a woman so full of humility and haya, that she covered herself like no other woman covered, and due to her we have been granted the gift of tasbih-faatimah.

"It is reported on the authority of Ali that Faatimah had corns in her hand because of working at the hand-mill. There had fallen to the lot of Allah's Messenger ﷺ some prisoners of war. She came to the Prophet ﷺ but she did not find him (in the house). She met A'isha and informed her (about her hardship). When the Messenger of Allah ﷺ came home, A'isha told him about the visit of Faatimah. He ﷺ went to them (Faatimah and her family). They had gone to their beds.

'Ali further (reported): We tried to stand up (as a mark of respect) but Allah's Messenger ﷺ said: Keep to your beds, and he sat amongst us and I felt the coldness of his feet upon my chest. He then said: May I not direct you to something better than what you have asked for? When you go to your bed, you should recite Takbir (Allah-u-Akbar) thirty-four times and Tasbih (Subhan Allah) thirty-three times and Tahmid (al-Hamdu li-Allah) thirty-three times, and that is better than the servant for you."

(Sahih Muslim)

This has been given the name of Tasbih-Faatimah, and we are encouraged to recite these words of praise, after every prayer and before sleeping.

Allahu Akbar - 34, Subhan Allah - 33, Alhamdulilah - 33.

The Prophet ﷺ said:

"Indeed Faatimah is but a part of me, I am harmed by what harms her and I am uncomfortable by what makes her uncomfortable."

(Jami At-Tirmidhi)

Umm Sulaym

The mother of the famous sahabi Anas bin Malik.

She was a devoted believer and dedicated her son Anas into the service of the Prophet Muhammad ﷺ since when he was very small.

The companion Talha radi Allahu anhu (prior to his accepting

Islam) requested to marry her after the death of her first husband. However she told him he would have to accept Islam first. He later accepted Islam and married her.

It was said that her Mahr (dowry) was the most valuable Mahr as she had kept Islam as her Mahr.

This is powerful dear sisters. She did not request riches or rubies although that was very much her right, but she chose the most valuable thing of all, the Deen.

Her family was very dear to the Messenger of Allah ﷺ and she would send gifts of dates and milk to the Prophet's family and the Messenger of Allah ﷺ would often take naps in her house.

She would collect his glittering beads of sweat in a little vial as he slept and would mix it in with her perfume. On one occasion the Prophet Muhammad ﷺ placed his lips over the mouth of her water pouch and drank from it. She then cut the mouth off and preserved it for barakah (blessings).

These narrations alone show her level of devotion for the Prophet of Allah ﷺ.

Many a narration in the books of ahadith record that our beloved Muhammad ﷺ prayed for her and her family and had special regard for her.

Umm sulaym loved learning and her thirst for knowledge made her unafraid to ask questions on sensitive fiqh issues, that other women were too ashamed to ask. Thus she encouraged women to ask when they were unsure on matters in the Deen and had questions, regardless of how personal the questions they had were.

She was courageous and was seen tending to the wounded on the battlefield of Uhud along with A'isha.

It was narrated by Anas ibn Malik:

When the Messenger of Allah went on an expedition, he took Umm Sulaym, and he had some women of the Ansar who supplied water and tended to the wounded.

(Sunan Abi Dawud)

Umm Sulaym was an extremely generous and active woman amongst the companions, often feeding and aiding the believers. We pray Allah rewards her tenfold for all her generosity and love.

Umm Umarah- Nusaybah daughter of Ka'b.

Umm Umarah had a very special place amongst the female companions and Allah Honoured her in many ways. She was from amongst the first Ansari women from Madinah to accept Islam and was an amazingly brave, strong, believing woman who accompanied her husband and two sons to many of the battles during the life of the Prophet ﷺ.

Renowned for her bravery on the battlefield, her loyalty and her patience, she was a model of strength for muslim women then and continues to be, for many of us today.

Her role was usually to tend to the wounded but in the battle of Uhud when many Muslim men had fled the battlefield, she shielded the Prophet ﷺ, and took up arms to defend him. Without hesitation she flung her body in the line of fire using it as a shield, and fought off the enemy using both a sword and bow and arrows; blocking many who were attempting to kill the Messenger of Allah.

Her courageousness earned her the respect of all the companions and she was praised and held in high regard by all. It is said that in whichever direction the Prophet ﷺ turned, he saw her protecting him.

She was a warrior in every sense of the word and she encouraged her sons to fight in the way of Allah. She received 13 wounds on the day of Uhud, and 11 in the Battle of Yamama where she also lost her hand. A woman who showed more bravery than many men and who never hesitated once to defend the Prophet ﷺ with her life.

She questioned things in regards to gender mentions in the Holy Qur'an and Allah Honoured her with a reply by sending down verse 35 of Surah Al Ahzab.

She herself narrates that she came to the Prophet ﷺ and said:

"I do not see but that everything is for men, and I do not see anything being mentioned for the women."

So this ayah was revealed: "Indeed, the Muslim men and Muslim women, the believing men and believing women, the obedient men and obedient women, the truthful men and truthful women, the patient men and patient women, the humble men and humble women, the charitable men and charitable women, the fasting men and fasting women, the men who guard their private parts and the women who do so, and the men who remember Allah often and the women who do so - for them Allah has prepared forgiveness and a great reward."

(Jami' At-Tirmidhi)

The Messenger of Allah ﷺ was pleased with and prayed for her and her family and invoked Allah's blessings upon them. In turn, the sahaba also praised her and held her in high esteem.

Asma- Daughter of Abu Bakr

She was the daughter of the famous companion Abu Bakr Siddiq, and was brought up in an atmosphere of purity and devotion to the Messenger of Allah ﷺ. She was one of the prominent believing women and is often mentioned in ahadith.

Asma accepted Islam when she was still very young and was raised as a righteous Muslimah. She was honoured with the great responsibility of keeping the secret of the Prophet ﷺ's migration to Madinah with her father and she helped them prepare for the journey.

She said:

"I prepared the provision bag for the Prophet ﷺ in the house of Abu Bakr (her father) when he wanted to emigrate to Madinah. We did not find anything with which to tie his bag or waterskin. I said to my father, "By Allah, I cannot find anything to tie with except my belt." He said, "Tear it in two and tie the waterskin with one and the bag with the other."

That is what she did and since then she was known as Dhatun-Nitaqayn (she of the two belts).

(Sahih al Bukhari)

Asma did not lead an easy life. She was married to Az-Zubayr who was one of the ashra mubashara (ten companions promised paradise). He was a very righteous man, however, he had neither land, nor wealth when he married her and her days were spent in hard labour. Yet she was modest and did not complain.

Elder sister to A'isha radi allaha anha, she often would come to her to ask about different rulings. She was the reliable narrator of 58 ahadith and this shows she was a woman with knowledge and understanding of the religion, like her sister. Asma was a generous woman and often spent her wealth in the path of Allah ﷺ. She was brave and bore her hardships with patience and her life teaches us many lessons. May Allah be pleased with her.

Sumayyah, Mother of Ammar Bin Yassir

Sumayyah, may Allah be pleased with her, was a strong brave woman and became the first martyr in the cause of Islam. She, her husband Yasir and their son Ammar, were slaves and some of the earliest converts to Islam.

When the mushrikeen (polytheists) of Makkah found out that Sumayyah and her family had accepted Islam, they mercilessly inflicted torture upon them. They dragged them over the hot sands of the desert, where they tied them up and tortured them relentlessly.

Abu Jahl subjugated her and her family to extremely savage brutality, yet she stayed firm in her imaan even whilst her body was undergoing excruciatingly painful torture.

Realising she would not renounce her faith in Allah and his Messenger ﷺ, he drove his spear through her and made her the first martyr in Islam.

Shortly after, her husband Yassir was killed and made a shaheed (martyr); their son Ammar was relentlessly tortured and made to watch as his parents were subjugated to such horror and unimaginable cruelty.

The Messenger of Allah ﷺ, gave her and her family the glad tidings of a meeting place in Jannah.

She was so firm in her belief that no amount of pain inflicted upon her made her renounce her faith. Islam was her life and she died for it, allowing her name to live on always.

Saffiyah- Daughter of Abdul Mutallib

This amazing woman was the paternal aunt of the Prophet Muhammad ﷺ, daughter of Abdul Mutallib and full sister of Hamza radi Allahu anhu. She was a woman with many sides to her. She had a strong stern approach and personality and she took the Deen very seriously. She was very strict with her sons to the point that other people got involved and asked her to be gentle with them. To which she would reply that she wanted to make men out of her sons, men that would never fear or surrender to any of the creation and only to their Creator.

She succeeded in her efforts and her sons grew up to be strong and fearless in body and soul.

Her son Az- Zubayr became Muslim before her and she would challenge him on his reversion, but she was unable to sway him and he was firm in his belief. She herself accepted Islam later on, on the same day her brother Hamza radi Allahu anhu accepted Islam.

She is a key figure and had many praiseworthy vital roles that she played at the time of the Messenger ﷺ. Of these roles, one of her most famous was the key part she played in the Battle of the Trenches, otherwise known as Ghazwa-e-Khandaq. She was a fighter and was as fearless as her brother Hamza. She had afterall, been raised in a household of warriors.

During the Battle of the Trenches, the Messenger of Allah ﷺ, left the women and children in a fortress at a little distance from where the main battle was taking place. He left them there and appointed Hassan bin Thabit radi Allahu anhu to stay with them, as he was severely ill and was unable to take part in the main battle.

A man from the opposing army climbed the fortress until he was able to see where the women and children were and scout the area. This endangered the women and Saffiyah upon seeing this, asked Hassan to rise up and kill him but he replied that if he could do so he would have been with the Prophet ﷺ and would not have been assigned to look after the women. He was too weak to move.

She decided to take matters in her own hands and so she rose up behind the scout and hit him across the head. She then threw him from the walls at the army below, who were waiting to hear back from their scout in the hope to attack and take over the fortress. The army upon seeing their man flung from the battlements, abandoned their plans of attack as they thought there must be an army inside the fortress and they dispersed. Thus, single handedly Saffiyah had managed to protect all of the women, children and even the men who had stayed back from the war.

This is how courageous she was even in her old age.

There are many more examples of her bravery and Islam encourages us women to be as she was, and to learn how to defend ourselves.

Other than her bravery she was also known as a very educated fluent poet and often spoke in poetic verses, which indicated a high level of intellect.

She lived till the caliphate of Umar radi Allahu anhu and was a strong leading figure amongst the companions till her last days.

May we all benefit from the stories of her life.

My beautiful sister, these are just a few of the blessed women who many of us are fortunate enough to share a name with. So why should we not try to emulate them in their character too.

These are the role models we should be taking as our own. They were women of substance, each one filled with the desire to please Allah ﷻ, and to excel in matters of Deen. Pious women with the goal to be loved by Allah and His angels and reach the highest levels of Jannah.

They each had an extraordinary impact on the life of the Messenger of Allah ﷺ, often providing the comfort that only a woman can give. From the beginning of his mission with Khadija to the day he passed away in the lap of A'isha; Islam flourished in the lap of women and the wives of the Prophet of Allah ﷺ have brought great value to Islam, and have benefited the believers immensely. Many verses of the Holy Qur'an were revealed due to them, and many ahadith have been preserved due to their careful attention to detail.

Each of these shimmering diamonds, even though they were very different in character, they had many things in common; their love for the Deen, their eagerness to please Allah ﷻ and His Messenger ﷺ, their selflessness in the cause of Islam, their strength and their inner and outer modesty.

May Allah ﷻ grant us the same thirst to be amongst the pious and grant us modesty in our hearts, appearance, tongue and actions, ameen.

Allah ﷻ has honoured women in Islam with many achievements in which some have surpassed the greatest men of their time.

The first believer was a woman, the first martyr was a woman, one of the first scholars and great transmitters of hadith was a woman!

Women have always been pioneers and at the fore- front of Islamic communities. We have so much to give and so much to contribute to in our societies, and have been doing so since the creation of our mother Hawa.

Many of the most influential scholars were brought up in an Islamic environment and pushed to study the Deen when they were very young by their mothers.

Let us be amongst those who are of a benefit to people and whose achievements force people to think well of Islam. We are the flag bearers of our religion and we must work towards excellence in all of our affairs.

The first step towards this is to learn more about our Deen and to implement what we learn, in ourselves, in our households and then in our communities.

May Allah ﷻ make us from those He is pleased with. May He grant us the piety of Maryam alayhi slaam, the modesty of Faatimah, the patience of Hajar, the honour of Khadija, the bravery of Umm Umara, the knowledge of A'isha, and most of all the complete reliance in Allah ﷻ that all of these women possessed. Allahumma ameen.

Here's to strong women
May we know them
May we be them
May we raise them.

CHAPTER 2

What does it mean to be a woman in Islam?

We hear the rhetoric "Islam oppresses women" all too often, so let us explore the status and position Islam actually has given us. Are we oppressed as they say we are? Do we have no voice and are we thought of as the inferior gender according to Islamic teachings?

Women are addressed in the Noble Qur'an and in ahadith, right beside men. Islam addresses us equally, and does not discriminate. Men and women are equal in value and responsibility; the distinction is made only on the basis of piety and righteousness.

"O mankind, indeed We have created you from male and female and made you peoples and tribes that you may know one another. Indeed, the most noble of you in the sight of Allah is the most righteous of you. Indeed, Allah is Knowing and Acquainted."

(Surah Al-Hujurat, verse 13)

My lovely sister, we are held in high esteem and respect and Islam honours us. Our Deen corrects the opinions found in other religions where they blame Eve for the fall of Adam and claim that she enticed Adam to eat the fruit from the forbidden tree, thus claiming that she is the one to blame for mans downfall from heaven. For this reason they view women as inherently evil and easily misled.

Firstly, Islam teaches us that Prophets are pure and free from sin, so we do not regard Adam's action of eating from the fruit a sin, rather we consider it a mistake and the ultimate qadr of Allah.

Secondly according to Islamic teachings, women are not the

cause of ill fortune and downfall of men.

The Holy Qur'an clearly tells us that each individual is liable for their own deeds. A woman is not more blameworthy for her deeds than a man is.

"And every soul earns not [blame] except against itself, and no bearer of burdens will bear the burden of another. Then to your Lord is your return, and He will inform you concerning that over which you used to differ."

(Surah Al-An'am, verse 164)

If anything, Islam has placed emphasis on and instructed men to honour and respect women; as an individual, a stranger, a daughter, sister, wife, and a mother.

Women who have no knowledge of their rights can not claim them, so let us educate ourselves on some of the rights we have been granted by Allah ﷻ, and then let us look at the rights others have and why these rights are so important.

KNOW your rights my sister and KNOW the rights others have over you. Once you know them, you can educate others on them.

"The empowered woman is powerful beyond measure and beautiful beyond description."

As a daughter and a sister:

Abu Sa'eed Al-Khudri narrated that, The Messenger of Allah ﷺ said:
"Whoever has three daughters, or three sisters, or two daughters, or two sisters and he keeps good company with them and fears Allah regarding them, then Paradise is for him."

(Jami At-Tirmidhi)

Allah ﷻ has granted us dignity and men have been ordered to treat us with respect and kindness. Everyone's life is considered sacred in Islam but special emphasis has been placed on treating women gently and with kindness.

Pre Islam, the birth of a son was considered a blessing and the birth of a daughter was considered a shame. Fathers would bury their daughters alive with no remorse and this was the custom. This barbaric treatment was extremely common.

This is the lack of value they had for a females life.

The Prophet ﷺ came and firmly condemned and put a stop to this evil practice and said:

"Whoever has a daughter and he does not bury her alive, nor humiliates her, nor prefers his sons over her, he will enter Paradise due to her."

(Sunan Abi Dawud)

In multiple ahadith we have been described as a huge blessing for our parents. They could enter Heaven just from treating us well and raising us with care and love.

The better the action the better the reward, and what better reward than Heaven.

Narrated by `Aisha:

"A lady along with her two daughters came to me asking me (for some alms), but she found nothing with me except one date which I gave to her and she divided it between her two daughters, and then she got up and went away. Then the Prophet ﷺ came in and I informed

him about this story. He said, "Whoever is in charge of (put to test by) these daughters and treats them generously, then they will act as a shield for him from the (Hell) Fire."

(Sahih al Bukhari)

Unfortunately even today in some cultures around the world, the birth of a son is more celebrated than the birth of a daughter.

This is why it is so important to know the value Islam has placed on these matters, because no culture is greater than religion. Culture and religion are often considered one and the same by some people, and it is very important to make the distinction clear.

Alhamdulilah my sister, you can gently correct people now if you see them showing disdain at the birth of a baby girl.

Remind them to be grateful that Allah has blessed them with a healthy baby, how many blessings their daughter has brought with her and how if treated well and given love and care she will be their ticket to Jannah in sha Allah. You will receive the rewards of spreading and teaching the sayings of our beloved Prophet ﷺ, and they will be reminded of the great blessing Allah ﷻ has bestowed upon them.

As a wife:

It often can appear to people that western society takes the lead in women empowerment, however traditionally it has been quite the contrary. For example, in the West traditionally the wife gives up her maiden name and acquires her husband's name after marriage.

This stems from a 14th Century Norman tradition, that after marriage the woman is now the property of the male and belongs to him and her identity revolves around being his wife. Over the years the thought process behind it has changed but the tradition has remained the same, with the majority of women abandoning their birth name and adopting their husband's name. In western traditional understanding, after marriage a husband and wife become one and so the woman takes her husband's name, and they say this symbolises unity.

In Islam however, as women we are encouraged to keep our birth surname rather than change it to our husband's name after marriage. This is because according to the Islamic perspective, we are our own person and we have our own identity. This does not change after marriage. Marriage in Islam does not mean that we are now the property of someone else, or that we have now become one with our husband. Rather it means, that we each keep our own individuality and the Noble Qur'an indicates that marriage is an equal partnership involving the man and the woman. We each have our own roles to play and our own rights; in turn this fosters a loving and stable relationship, with spiritual harmony between the spouses.

Allah ﷻ says in the Holy Qur'an:

"And of His signs is that He created for you from yourselves mates that you may find tranquillity in them; and He placed between you affection and mercy. Indeed in that are signs for a people who give thought."

(Surah Ar-Rum, verse 21)

My dear sister, Islam also gives us the right to choose our spouse and our parents are not allowed to marry us to anyone without our consent. This may not seem like something big now, but was unheard of at the time.

Unfortunately in some cultures women are forced to marry

and nobody stops it from happening. This is often because not enough people are educated about the rights Islam has given us. The girls who have no knowledge of their rights feel pressured and are forced to comply and their opinion on the matter is often suppressed in these circumstances.

In these cases it is culture that is oppressive not religion. It is extremely important to make that distinction because unfortunately, many people are leaving Islam for things that they associate with the Deen, when in actual fact it is the negative aspects of their culture and harmful parenting that is to blame.

Some parents due to their own lack of knowledge believe they have the right to have the last say and their daughter should just quietly accept whatever they wish for her.

Abu Huraira radi Allahu anhu reported Allah's Messenger ﷺ as having said:

"A woman without a husband (or divorced or a widow) must not be married until she is consulted, and a virgin must not be married until her permission is sought."

They asked the Prophet of Allah ﷺ, "How can her consent be solicited?"

He ﷺ said: "She keeps silent."

(Sahih Muslim)

We are given security in marriage and protection and we are allowed to grow and explore our own individuality. Our Deen teaches men to take care of us and our needs, and to give us our rights; in return we respect our husband's rights over us. It is a balanced partnership and if everyone followed the teachings of Islam as they should be followed, respected the boundaries set, and gave each other the rights that Allah ﷻ has given us all, the world would be a much better place and there would be less issues in all aspects of life.

Together with all the required provisions for our welfare and security at the time of marriage, Islam has also given us the right to a Mahr.

The Mahr is a marriage gift given by the husband to his wife and it symbolises his love for her and his intention to care for and provide for her. The ownership of the Mahr is only for the wife, not for the family or the father of the wife to take. It is hers alone to do with as she wishes.

Before Islam, Arabs had some customs that were very demeaning towards women, some of which I have already mentioned. Another custom was that of inheriting wives. If a man passed away, his relatives had the right to inherit his wife along with his possessions. Once again you find this idea that women were just the property of men. If any of them wished, they could marry her or they could marry her to someone else or even prevent her from marrying altogether. They felt they had the right to control every aspect of her life how they wished.

Islam came and gave a voice to the wife, which before Islam was never heard, and the Messenger of Allah ﷺ put a stop to this barbaric treatment.

Allah says in the Holy Qur'an,

"O you who have believed, it is not lawful for you to inherit women by compulsion. And do not make difficulties for them in order to take [back] part of what you gave them unless they commit a clear immorality. And live with them in kindness. For if you dislike them - perhaps you dislike a thing and Allah makes therein much good."

(Surah An-Nisa, verse 19)

It was narrated from Ibn 'Abbas radi Allahu anhu that the Prophet ﷺ said:

"The best of you is the one who is best to his wife, and I am the best of you to my wives."

(Sunan Ibn Majah)

It was narrated from 'Abdullah bin 'Amr that: the Messenger of Allah ﷺ said:

"The best of you are those who are best to their womenfolk."

(Sunan ibn Majah)

Abu Hurairah narrated that The Messenger of Allah ﷺ said:

"The most complete of the believers in faith, is the one with the best character among them. And the best of you are those who are best to your women."

(Jami At-Tirmidhi)

Many many ahadith have been recorded on this topic. Our beloved Prophet ﷺ, knew that there were and would be men who treated women extremely poorly. This is the reason he emphasised the importance of having good treatment towards women.

In an ideal world, we would hope that men would do exactly that. That they would treat all women but especially those who are vulnerable to them e.g. their wives and daughters kindly and with care, and would give them the rights Islam has already given them. However, unfortunately we do not live in an ideal world. Some men will go against the teachings of Islam and twist rulings to their own advantage due to their misogynistic cultural upbringing and false sense of superiority.

My dear sister, it is important to realise that in cases like that it is culture and the men involved who are to blame. Religion is not to blame for the misguided actions of men, as religion is clear on these matters.

They will be held accountable for all their wrongs on the Day of Reckoning, just like we will.

It is also important to state the obvious, that not all men misuse their authority. Many men honour women and do not transgress their boundaries in regards to them. They are kind and fear Allah ﷻ in the treatment of their women, and in all of their affairs. These men should be respected in turn and it is unfair to place them in the same category as the men who are oppressive, or to label them as such.

Islam does not teach us to hate each other so we should be careful not to place unwarranted dislike on innocent parties. There is no "women versus men" in Islam. May Allah ﷻ reward all those who treat their women and their families well.

I pray you and all the sisters reading this are granted respect, love and safety in your homes. I pray Allah shields you from all harm and keeps you in His Protection.

Ameen.

As a mother:

When a woman becomes a mother, this is one avenue through which Allah ﷺ raises her status. Children have been ordered again and again to honour their parents and to treat them with kindness and patience.

Allah ﷺ says in the Holy Qur'an,

"And your Lord has decreed that you not worship except Him, and to parents, good treatment. Whether one or both of them reach old age [while] with you, say not to them [so much as], "uff," and do not repel them but speak to them a noble word."

(Surah Al-Isra, 23)

Special emphasis has been placed upon treating mothers well because of the difficulties a mother goes through; from pregnancy to the pains of labour, breast feeding and then raising her child. The differences pregnancy brings to her physically and how it can affect her mentally, during and after giving birth.

Many times the Holy Qur'an mentions the status of both the father and the mother in general, but then more details are given in regards to the mother.

"And We have enjoined upon man, to his parents, good treatment. His mother carried him with hardship and gave birth to him with hardship, and his gestation and weaning [period] is thirty months. [He grows] until, when he reaches maturity and reaches [the age of] forty years, he says, "My Lord, enable me to be grateful for Your favour which You have bestowed upon me and upon my parents and to work righteousness of which You will approve and make righteous for me my offspring. Indeed, I have repented to You, and indeed, I am of the

Muslims."

(Surah Al Ahqaf, verse 15)

*"And We have enjoined upon man [care] for his parents.
His mother carried him, [increasing her] in weakness
upon weakness, and his weaning is in two years. Be
grateful to Me and to your parents; to Me is the [final]
destination."*

(surah Luqmaan, verse 14)

In our Faith, a woman's struggles are not brushed under
the carpet. They are mentioned in detail. Each struggle is
acknowledged, heard and rewarded.

Allah ﷻ talks about a mother's struggles and pains in detail,
emphasising how much of a sacrifice child bearing is and how
much children in turn should value their mother for these
sacrifices.

Great mothers of Prophets have been recognised and the
struggles they have faced for their children have been recorded
in the Holy Qur'an and praised.

This includes the likes of Maryam, the mother of Isa alayhi
slaam, who endured the pains of pregnancy and birth in private
and alone, and then came back to her people who shamed her
even though she was the purest of the pure.

Also the courage of Hajar alayhi slaam who was left in the
middle of the dry, hot desert with her baby and no food and
drink; who ran up one mountain and then another to search for
signs of water to quench her babe's thirst.

And the sacrifice and patience of Musa alayhi slaam's mother,
who placed him in a basket and let the basket float upon the river
not knowing where it would end up, all to protect him from

being killed.

These events show the extent to which mothers are prepared to go in order to save their child's life. Women go through so many physical and emotional pains for the sake of their children and Allah has honoured them in return. The least we can do is to give them the respect and devotion they deserve.

Our beloved prophet Muhammad ﷺ taught the sahaba through action, and was a living example of the level of love and care we should all show our mothers.

Abu Huraira reported that a person said:

"Allah's Messenger, who amongst the people is most deserving of my good treatment?"

He ﷺ replied: "Your mother, again your mother, again your mother, then your father, then your nearest relatives according to the order (of nearness)."

(Sahih Muslim)

In Al-Adab Al-Mufrad the above hadith is recorded in these words,

"The Prophet ﷺ was asked, "Messenger of Allah, to whom should I be dutiful?" 'Your mother,' he replied. He was asked, 'Then whom?' 'Your mother,' he replied. He was asked, 'Then whom?' 'Your mother,' he replied. He was asked, 'Then whom?' He ﷺ replied, 'Your father.'"

(This hadith is also found in Sahih Bukhari, Sahih Muslim and other great books of hadith).

Ibn Salamah As-Sulami narrated that the Prophet ﷺ said:

"I enjoin each one to honour his mother, I enjoin each one to honour his mother, I enjoin each one to honour his mother (three times), I enjoin each one to honour his guardian who is taking care of him, even if he is causing him some annoyance."

(Sunan ibn Majah)

The Messenger of Allah ﷺ often repeated himself when asked about a mother's status. This is because repetition gives emphasis on the importance of the speech, and it helps the listener memorise and then implement what is being said.

My dear sister, too many of us lose our patience with our parents and especially with our mothers. We are annoyed easily by little things they say and do. Even if we feel like we are in the right and our mothers are in the wrong, it is our duty to respect them and not to talk back to them. How would we want our children to speak to and treat us? We should treat our mothers the way we would like to be treated by our own children.

We can not repay our mothers ever for all their sacrifices; the difficulty which they went through to carry us inside their womb for months and then all the pain and hardship of giving birth to us. Then the sleepless nights and feeding and bathing which all take time, effort and patience.

"Sa'id ibn Abi Burda said, "I heard my father say that Ibn 'Umar saw a Yemeni man going around the House while carrying his mother on his back, saying, 'I am your humble camel. If her mount is frightened, I am not frightened.' Then he asked, 'Ibn 'Umar? Do you think that I have repaid her?' He replied, 'No, not even for a single groan"

(Al-Adab Al-Mufrad)

He was carrying his mother on his back, whilst doing tawaf of the Holy Kaabah in the heat of the Arabian sun, and he was told he had not even repaid her for a single groan that had escaped her lips when she was giving birth to him.

That is a mother's status. Even if we spent all our life in their service we can not repay them.

In Islam, wet nurses are also given the status of a mother.

The Prophet ﷺ had a wet nurse by the name of Halima Saadiyah and treated her with the same love and care that was given to birth mothers. The way he treated her is the closest we can get to seeing his prophetic teachings regarding mothers in action as his birth mother Aaminah had passed away when he was just a child.

This respect was shown not just to Halima, but also extended to her husband and her family. This shows that even a woman's milk is given so much importance and value that the wet nurse is elevated because of it.

On the occasions that Halima Saadiyah did visit the Messenger of Allah ﷺ, he got up for her and her husband and sat them on his shawl as a sign of utmost respect.

It was narrated by Umar ibn as-Sa'ib:

"One day when the Messenger of Allah peace be upon him was sitting, his foster-father came forward. He ﷺ spread out of a part of his garment and he sat on it. Then his mother came forward to him and he ﷺ spread out the other side of his garment and she sat on it. Again, his foster-brother came forward. The Messenger of Allah stood for him and seated him before himself."

(Sunan Abi Dawud)

There is a lesson in this on how to treat our parents and the respect to show them whilst being in their company. Give up your seat and show them the utmost respect.

Also that same level of respect extends yet again to your aunt, your mother's sister.

Al-Bara' bin 'Azib (May Allah be pleased with them) reported:

I heard the Prophet (peace be upon him) saying: "A mother's sister is equivalent to (real) mother (in status)".

(Riyadh As Saaliheen)

My dear sister, as a daughter, sister, wife, mother, aunt and most importantly as a beautiful Muslim woman; YOU are respected. You have rights in Islam and You are honoured in the sight of Allah. May you never find yourself in a situation where your rights are being violated.

For too long Islam has been blamed for the flaws of men and the flaws of different cultural practices. This is a great injustice to our religion.

Islam has granted women fundamental rights to life, property and to voice our opinions just as men have been. This knowledge is powerful and allows us to exercise our rights within the boundaries of religion.

Unfortunately many Muslim women have lived oppressed subdued lives because their men have forcefully taken control of all finances and sought control over them.

Many have been bullied into silence whilst their men abuse their authority over them and repeatedly tell them that this is what Islam expects of them.

Women have been denied access to mosques and have had

their finances controlled and forcefully taken. They have faced domestic violence and have all too often been the subject of marital rape and abuse. Honour killings and forced marriages, the barring of education and social and economic exclusions; all committed in the name of Islam and this is the greatest deception and injustice of all.

There will always be those who twist the teachings of religion, but as long as we know what our rights are nobody can overpower us.

Our Deen has taught us a woman has rights of her own. The Messenger of Allah ﷺ taught us that women are entitled to education, wealth, earnings, a voice in their communities and are not to be excluded from mosques and that men should fear their treatment of them.

We are very much a part of society and contribute in every way. Allah has given us strengths that are different to the strengths men have been given. We have more forgiving hearts and a gentler approach and we can use these wisely. The closer we are to our Deen, the more we can improve on ourselves, and can bring our families towards the deen.

Women attending the Masajid in the time of the Messenger of Allah ﷺ

It was narrated by Ibn Umar:

The Prophet said, "If your women ask permission to go to the mosque at night, allow them."

(Sahih al Bukhari)

There were believing women who used to attend prayers in the masjid during the life of the Messenger of Allah ﷺ. There are ahadith which describe them sitting inside as a group, and the Prophet ﷺ passing by them.

They were allowed to attend when they wished and their men were forbidden from preventing them from going out to the masjid.

Many mosques in the U.K and around the world do not have sufficient facilities for women, and women have been turned away from the door.

This goes against the teachings of the Messenger of Allah ﷺ and the clear wording of multiple ahadith, where men have specifically been addressed and commanded not to forbid women from going to the mosque. Women have the right to attend circles of knowledge and to go to the mosque when they wish. The houses of worship are open to us, just as they are to men.

The Prophet ﷺ did not exclude women in matters of religion and worship.

Even a strong minded sahabi like Umar radi Allahu anhu, who personally preferred for women to pray in their homes, did not forbid his wives from attending the masajid. If the Messenger of Allah ﷺ said it was permissible for them to enter, he knew the words of the Prophet ﷺ were the only authority that mattered on the subject.

Narrated by Ibn Umar:

One of the wives of Umar ibn Al-Khattab (radi Allahu anhu) used to offer the Fajr and the Isha prayer in congregation in the Mosque. She was asked why she had come out for the prayer as she knew that Umar disliked it, and he has great ghaira (self-respect).

She replied: "What prevents him from stopping me from

this act?" The other replied, "The statement of Allah's Messenger: "Do not stop Allah's women-slaves from going to Allah's mosques" prevents him."

(Sahih al Bukhari)

Ibn Umar also reported:

Grant permission to women for going to the mosque in the night. His son who was called Waqid said: "But then they would make mischief.(We will not let them go)"

Ibn Umar said that he thumped his son's chest and said: "I am narrating to you the hadith of the Messenger of Allah ﷺ, and you say "No"

(Sahih Muslim)

From these reports it is clear to see the position the sahaba held upon the matter of women entering masajid.

Women are part of the community and should have their own space to worship Allah in the houses of worship.

A gentle reminder to my sisters that it is important to ensure that when attending places of worship we try to follow correct etiquette in our behaviour and dress. Attending masajid beautified, wearing tight clothing, make-up and perfume is not permissible, and acts as a distraction and hinders our spirituality.

Our purpose when attending prayers in the mosque is to worship Allah and focus on cleansing our heart and drawing closer to Him. There is no benefit in beautifying ourselves before we attend. Rather this is a trick of shaytan.

It was narrated from Zainab Ath-Thaqafiyyah that:

The prophet ﷺ said: "Any one of you (women) who wants to go out to the Masjid, should not go near any perfume."

(Sunan An-Nasa'l)

Narrated by A'isha:

Had Allah's Messenger known what the women were doing, he would have forbidden them from going to the mosque, as the women of Bani Isra'il had been forbidden.

Yahya bin Sa'id (a sub narrator) asked 'Amra (another sub narrator), "Were the women of Bani Isra'il forbidden?"

She replied, "Yes"

(Sahih al Bukhari)

'Amra, daughter of Abd al-Rahman, reported:

I heard A'isha, the wife of the Messenger of Allah say: "If the Messenger of Allah had seen what new things the women have introduced (in their way of life) he would have definitely prevented them from going to the mosque, as the women of Bani Isra'il were prevented."

(Sahih Muslim)

Masajid must have the capacity and facilities to cater for women as they do for men, and as women, we must ensure that we are not beautifying and perfuming ourselves before attending prayers in the house of Allah. If we cover ourselves appropriately and fear Allah, then it is permissible for us to attend.

If prayer time is passing and for some reason you do not have a correct covering, and need to pray, please do not take the above as a reason not to pray at all. In this situation it is better for you to attend the masjid. Similarly many newly practising muslims are encouraged to attend classes in masajid to grow closer to the Deen, and every mosque should have a supply of suitable covering and hijabs for attendees to use when needed.

However, if your home is nearby it is better to pray at home.

The right of Inheritance

We have been granted the right of inheritance and all our wealth is ours alone to do with as we wish.

We have this advantage over men as men are obligated to spend on their women and support and provide for them. Their wealth is not theirs alone to spend upon just themselves.

However Islam is balanced and for this reason, males have been given a bigger share in inheritance than women have. The male inherits more but is responsible financially for other females; daughters, wives, mothers, and sisters. The female inherits less but she keeps it all for investment and financial security and has no obligation to spend any part of it even for her own sustenance (food, clothing, housing, medication, etc as this is the duty of her father, brother or husband to provide for her.

Islam is beautiful and just and empowers women, providing them with financial security and the right to spend their wealth however they wish.

Allah says in the Noble Qur'an:

"For men is a share of what the parents and close relatives leave, and for women is a share of what the parents and close relatives leave, be it little or much - an obligatory share.

Muslim women have been given these rights thirteen hundred years before the West recognised that these rights even existed.

We, as women, have many strengths and should be supported and encouraged to become the best version of ourselves.

My sister, these are the teachings of The Messenger of Allah ﷺ. We can not flourish when we are surrounded by abuse and are denied our basic rights.

May Allah protect everyone from the wrongful actions of those who abuse their power and grant them strength to overcome their difficulties.

Islam is a religion of balance and values equity between the genders. Where men have their rights, women have theirs. Each individual is to be respected regardless of gender and is to be treated justly. The comfort women bring to the home is matched with the safety a man provides for the family. Both are in union and create a stable balanced atmosphere.

5 THOUGHTS AND LESSONS FROM THIS CHAPTER TO PONDER UPON

1. Turn to Allah and pray to Him to help you in your affairs and your struggles. Prayer is the weapon of the believer and will aid you in every circumstance.

2. Know your rights! Educating yourself upon the rights Allah has granted you will make you strong and confident and will allow the love for the Deen to grow even more in your heart.

3. Women have a very special place in Islamic society. Cultural influences in Muslim countries which treat women badly and go against the teachings of Islam must

be discarded.

4.   Women are the twin halves and companions of men. For society to bloom and flourish, each must value the other and give each other due respect.

5.   Women must step forward and contribute to society. Do not rely solely on men to give. If they do not give, go out and get. Engage with believing women and create safe spaces for classes and to gather, pray and remember Allah. Create a strong sisterhood in your community.

The righteous Muslim woman is one who treats her family kindly and with love. Allah has granted her beauty and a gentle nature, which she can use to win the heart of all those whom she loves. With a little patience and knowledge of the rights others have over her, and the rights she has over them, she can bring peace to the home which can be felt by all.

Dear sister, learn to be content in your situation and listen to others, if you want others to listen to you. Strive to make your family happy as their happiness will result in your own happiness too. Remember that to compromise is not to lose, rather it is to prioritise that which will lead to something better.

*"A woman is not a commodity, or a toy for amusement,
But a real partner to a man.
She has rights of her own and deserves the utmost respect"*

CHAPTER 3

Cover girl or Covered Girl?

She learnt the value of her crown,

And the beauty in her long, loose gown

No longer would her insecurities bring her down

She's a Muslimah, a Queen in Islam

My respected sister, we live in a hyper sexualised society and in times in which promiscuity is considered freedom. Everywhere we look, we see women used as a tool to encourage the desires of men. Half naked women are advertised in the marketing of every product, their features air brushed and altered to cover and hide any "imperfections". Models pose alluringly in posters, adverts and magazines. Movements that originally began in order to improve the standing of women in society, are now reduced and corrupted by those who deem nudity to be the definition of empowerment.

This over sexualisation has led to an overall lack of respect for women. A woman is judged on her beauty to the point that many are altering their own pictures so much so that their pictures no longer reflect what they look like in real life. Others are risking their health and spending thousands of pounds as they turn to surgery in an attempt to look "beautiful".

Too many women have become a pawn in society's beauty game, spending all their time, effort and money on an ever changing ideal of beauty. This endless loop of chasing perfection has severe mental and physical ramifications, and gives birth to unhealthy obsessions; causing eating disorders like Anorexia and Bulimia, low self esteem and a distorted self image. This is incredibly damaging to the youth of today, and is leaving young sisters with depression and anxiety.

"Perfection is an impossible destination"

Chasing perfection in outward beauty will never make us happy, my dear sister. We will become increasingly unhappy and depressed if we place so much value on how we look. Islam has granted us protection and a means to combat these issues that stem from low self esteem and an inherent desire to fit in the crowd. Concepts like that of Hijab, liberate us from these expectations that society has of women.

When we meet someone new our initial impression is based on looks, and only after does personality, character, manners and level of intellect start to take on meaning.

However, when a woman is observing hijab and is covered, it forces people to look past her features and looks and instead focus on her personality, manners and brains first. This gives a non biased and more accurate opinion of her.

"She was beautiful, but in ways other than those girls in the magazines. She was beautiful for how she thought. She was beautiful for the sparkle in her eyes when she spoke about the Deen and the things she loved.

She was beautiful for her perseverance and her ability to make others smile.

No she wasn't beautiful for something as temporary as her looks, nor was she reduced to them.

She was beautiful right down to her soul."

As Muslims we believe everything our Creator Allah ﷻ has decreed for us is full of benefit and provides safety and security in society.

Allah ﷻ wants to see us happy and so He, with His Supreme Knowledge, has placed value on matters that are important. Of the matters that have immense value in the Deen are aspects such as modesty and hijab.

What is Modesty?

When modesty is mentioned the form that most commonly comes to mind is outward modesty, namely covering your body and avoiding clothing that reveals your body shape and skin colour.

However, modesty is not just confined to how we are dressed. Rather, it also applies to how we speak, what we say, how we act, and the things we surround ourselves with and look at. A modest person is one who covers what is supposed to be covered, avoids committing shameful actions, seeing shameful things, and whose speech is pure from inappropriate talk and language.

May Allah ﷻ make us from amongst such people, Ameen.

Allah loves modesty.

It was narrated from Ibn Abbas that the Prophet ﷺ, said to Ashajj 'Ansari:

"You have two characteristics that Allah likes: Forbearance and modesty"

(Sunan ibn Majah)

The Prophet ﷺ has also spoken about haya (modesty) being a part of faith.

It was narrated from Abu Huraira, that the Prophet peace be upon him said;

"Modesty (Al Haya) is a branch of faith."

(Sunan An Nasa'i)

There is another similar hadith recorded in Sunan An Nasa'I in these words,

"Faith has seventy odd branches and modesty (Al Haya) is a branch of faith."

So faith and modesty are intertwined and one can not be without the other.

In Islam, both men and women share the responsibility of modesty. It is up to each individual to guard their chastity and to control their desires, whether they take up that responsibility or not. It has been decreed.

It is interesting to note that Allah ﷻ has commanded men to maintain their haya, and lower their gaze, before he commanded both women and men to cover.

In Surah An Nur, verse 30, Allah ﷻ says:

"Tell the believing men to reduce [some] of their vision (lower their gaze) and guard their private parts. That is purer for them. Indeed, Allah is Acquainted with what they do."

For men, part of modesty is to lower their gaze and not ogle at women. This is an instruction for all men, and regardless of how a woman is dressed, men are supposed to keep their eyes to the ground and behave with honour. It is not from modesty for them to stare and feed their desires.

In verse 31 of Surah An Nur, directly following the instructions set for men, Allah ﷻ says,

"And tell the believing women to reduce [some] of their vision (lower their gaze) and guard their private parts and not expose their adornment except that which [necessarily] appears thereof and to wrap [a portion of] their head-covers over their chests and not expose their adornment except to their husbands, their fathers, their husbands' fathers, their sons, their husbands' sons, their brothers, their brothers' sons, their sisters' sons, their women, that which their right hands possess, or those male attendants having no physical desire, or children who are not yet aware of the private aspects of women. And let them not stamp their feet to make known what they conceal of their adornment. And turn to Allah in repentance, all of you, O believers, that you might succeed."

In this ayah, there are instructions to every believing woman on how to conduct themselves, and how to dress in public. This is from a woman's modesty.

She is to lower her gaze, just as men are to, and to cover what is required of a woman's body to be covered. She is told who her mahram are and who her non mahram are, and how to behave in public. She is not to stomp hard as she walks or walk in an alluring manner, as this draws unnecessary attention towards her. This is all from her haya and when these rulings are acted upon, it brings much betterment to society as a whole.

Both verses work together in harmony. To aid the believers in lowering their gaze, we also have been told to cover, one of the benefits of which is to prevent temptation. Both men and women have to respect the rulings set for us in the Deen and if each was to act upon them, there would be less ills and problems in society.

My dear sister, it is important to understand and internalise the fact that as believers, we do as Allah ﷻ commands without any "ifs" or "buts". We hear and obey and we do not delay in matters which Allah has specifically ordered for us to do. Yes there are many benefits to covering and acting upon the verses in the Noble Qur'an, however the main reason we do so, is simply because Allah, with His Supreme Divine wisdom, has told us to. We hear and we obey. By following Allah's rules we are worshipping Him, and for every act of worship we will earn reward.

In a school or university setting, we can not avoid the opposite gender altogether, nor are we expected to in the Deen. However there are guidelines in place which tell us how we should behave.

Being overly friendly and not observing the correct covering in the presence of male class fellows, students or co workers, is not permissible. Be polite and courteous but it is our responsibility not to overstep the limits the Deen has placed upon us. By all means have discussions and involve yourself in projects. Our voices are to be heard and we are encouraged to participate in society. However we can do so without compromising our Islamic values.

My dear sister, these rules are enforced in the Deen to protect us. To protect our limbs from falling into sin but also to protect our most valuable possession of all; our heart.

Every sin has an impact on our heart and causes it to become corrupted. Our lives are spent in trying to make sure we keep our heart as clean as possible. Each sin appears on our heart as a black dot. When we commit a minor sin, if we follow up that sin with a good deed, that good deed erases the sin, leaving our heart clean. This is from Allah's Mercy upon us.

Abu Hurairah narrated that:

the Messenger of Allah said: "Verily, when the slave (of Allah) commits a sin, a black spot appears on his heart. When he refrains from it, seeks forgiveness and repents, his heart is polished clean. But if he returns, it increases until it covers his entire heart. And that is the 'Ran' which Allah mentioned: 'Nay, but on their hearts is the Ran which they used to earn.'"

(Jami' At-Tirmidhi)

The heart will always have a connection with Allah. When we move further away from Him, the strings are pulled tighter and the distance brings us pain and heartbreak.

Reeling the heart strings back in towards the Love and Obedience of Allah gives us the relief our heart craves.

Accepting and living according to the rulings set down for us in the Deen, makes our connection to our Creator stronger, and leaves our heart healthy and happy. This is the true beauty in hearing and obeying.

Mahram and Non Mahram

A woman's mahram is a male who it is impermissible for her to marry and in front of whom she may remove her hijab. These are close family members such as her father, father in law, grandfathers, brothers, sons, grandsons, nephews, paternal and maternal uncles, husband's sons, and also any male who she or her mother has breastfed. They are sorted into categories as follows;

Mahram by ties of blood, Mahram by rada'ah (breast feeding) and Mahram by marriage.

Her husband is also her Mahram, however the ruling regarding him is slightly different as she is already married to him and can uncover her whole body infront of him.

What is Satar

Satar is an Arabic word and it refers to the body parts a believer is obliged to cover. For men, their satar starts from and includes their naval down to their knees, and for women, our satar is our whole body excluding our face, feet and hands, although there's a slight difference of opinion about this amongst the schools of thought.

One of the reasons behind this difference, is because a woman's body has more temptation in it for men, than a man's has for women and men have been created weak and find it harder to control their desires.

Sister, it is only in the presence of non mahram men that we must cover our satar. We do still have a type of satar to preserve in the presence of mahrams and other women, however it is different to that of non mahrams. It is not as strict.

A woman is allowed to have her neck, forearms, face, hair, and feet visible in front of male family members, the rest of her body must be covered in their presence.

In front of her husband she may uncover fully.

In front of other women, she must cover from her naval to her knees.

Bear in mind, this does not mean that a woman may sit with all her body parts showing or that we may look at each other's bodies without feeling shame. It is from haya and fitrah to cover ourselves and uncovering should not be normalised, even when amongst only women. We should still cover, however there is no harm in us showing that which appears itself whilst working or relaxing, and we are allowed to show each other our adornments.

Our eyes are the gateways to our heart and so we should always aim to expose ourselves to that which is beneficial for us to see, and should steer away from that which is impermissible and unnecessary to look at.

Living in the west and in an age of social media, we are surrounded by people of different faiths who do not see a problem with uncovering. For this reason we often are exposed to and see more than we would like to, however it is our responsibility to look away. Everything we look at has an impact on our heart and our spirituality, so we should aim to cover more rather than less even amongst women.

It is better for us not to uncover ourselves intentionally, or to make it a habit of doing so, and Allah ﷻ Knows best.

'Imran bin Hussain (May Allah be pleased with them) reported: The Messenger of Allah ﷺ said,

"Shyness does not bring anything except good."

(Al-Bukhari, Muslim, Riyad as-Salihin)

Shyness is a praiseworthy trait to have and it beautifies the person who embodies it in their character. The youth today are surrounded by people who are promiscuous and proud of their promiscuity and advertise it as if it is something to be proud of. Unfortunately many Muslims have adopted this attitude and it is damaging to their Deen. It has caused many youngsters to sin openly and feel no guilt in doing so.

Shyness has become strange and priding ourselves in immoral behaviour has become the norm. We need to reconnect with our fitrah and surround ourselves with positive influences and people who will have a positive effect on us. This will help us regain the sense of haya many of us have lost.

Anas ibn Malik radi allahu anhu reported, that our

beloved Prophet ﷺ said,

"Whenever there is modesty in a thing, it adorns it. Whenever there is outrage in a thing, it debases it."

(Al-Adab Al-Mufrad)

In some cultures more emphasis is placed upon a woman to be shy and modest in appearance and character, however according to Islamic values, shyness is for both genders. We have examples throughout our tradition of both men and women with unmatched levels of modesty.

The Prophets (peace be upon them) were filled with praise-worthy modesty, and great personalities amongst the Sahaba and pious predecessors (may Allah be pleased with them) are known for their haya. We have lessons on how they were modest outwardly and inwardly. Years and years have passed by, but stories of their modesty live on and will continue to do so.

Modesty the like of which Yusuf alayhi slaam had. It is said he was given half of all the beauty ever to have been created, but he kept his face covered out of shyness and to avoid fitnah coming towards him.

Another example is Ayyub alayhi slaam, who faced loss of wealth, loss of family and loss of good health for years, yet was too shy to ask Allah ﷻ for relief because of all the years of prosperity Allah ﷻ had granted him before the times of hardship that had befallen him. He was too shy to ask for relief because he felt he had been given so many blessings in his life.

Uthman ibn Affan radi allahu anhu, and his incredible shyness in how he dressed and in his character. He was known to be so modest that even the angels were shy in front of him.

It was narrated by 'Ali bin Abi Talib radi allahu anhu,

that the Messenger of Allah ﷺ said:

"May Allah have mercy upon Abu Bakr, he married me to his daughter, and he carried me to the land of Hijrah, and he freed Bilal with his wealth. May Allah have mercy upon 'Umar, he says the truth even if it is sour. The truth caused him to be left without a friend. May Allah have mercy upon 'Uthman, the angels are shy of him. May Allah have mercy upon 'Ali. O Allah! Place the truth with him wherever he turns."

(Jami' At- Tirmidhi)

Just imagine; angels who are pure and only do what Allah ﷺ commands them to do, even they are shy in the presence of Uthman radi allahu anhu. This is due to his incredible haya.

The higher level of modesty a person has, the more people are shy in their company. This is because modesty is a trait which rubs off on to the people around you. If your friends know you would not do an action out of modesty, it is more likely that they themselves would refrain from doing that action in front of you.

Bear in mind my dear sister, this is referring to praise worthy modesty not blame worthy modesty. Blame worthy modesty is shyness in telling people what is right and wrong and staying silent in the face of oppression and religious negligence. Being afraid of what people will say when you try to correct them, or tell them something of benefit, is not from haya. We are meant to enjoin the good and forbid the bad with firm resolve and confidence, but also with a healthy helping of good manners.

However, if you have praise worthy modesty, you will refrain from forbidden and disliked actions and will advise those around you to stay away from them too. This will then lead to the people around you being more aware of their actions, and feeling some sort of haya, whilst being in your company.

`Aisha may Allah be pleased with her, reported:

> *"Allah's Messenger ﷺ was lying in the bed in my*
> *apartment with his thigh uncovered and Abu Bakr*
> *sought permission to enter. It was given to him and he*
> *conversed in the same very state (the Prophet's thigh or*
> *shank uncovered). Then `Umar sought permission for*
> *entering and it was given to him and he conversed in*
> *that very state. Then `Uthman sought permission to*
> *enter; Allah's Messenger peace be upon him, sat down*
> *and he set right his clothes. Muhammad (one of the*
> *narrators) said: I do not say that it happened on the*
> *same day. He (`Uthman) then entered and conversed and*
> *as he went out, `Aisha said: Abu Bakr entered and you*
> *did not stir and did not observe much care (in arranging*
> *your clothes), then `Umar entered and you did not stir*
> *and did not arrange your clothes, then `Uthman entered*
> *and you got up and set your clothes right, so he (peace be*
> *upon him) said: Should I not show modesty to one whom*
> *even the Angels show modesty?"*

(Sahih Muslim)

SubhanAllah my sister, contemplate on how beautiful these ahadith are. Imagine being so full of haya, that the angels are shy of you and the best of creation shows you respect because of that. This is not to say that Abu Bakr and Umar radi Allahu anhuma were not modest, without a doubt they were; but Uthman radi Allahu anhu's modesty was unmatched.

May Allah ﷻ grant us all modesty and humility in our character.

Our beloved Prophet ﷺ, is the best of all creation and the

most modest out of all of Allah's Creations. Everything about his character is unmatched and nobody is more modest than his blessed self. He was perfect in every way.

Narrated by Abu Sa`id radi allahu anhu:

The Prophet peace be upon him, was more shy (from Haya': pious shyness from committing religious indiscretions) than a veiled virgin girl."

(Sahih al-Bukhari)

His wives and daughters and the sahaba, (May Allah be pleased with them all) had much modesty and this is due to their strong faith. The stronger your Imaan is, the more modest you are in all of your affairs.

The haya they had over the Deen is what encouraged them to command the good and forbid evil, and preserve Islam and the seerah in its full tradition.

Abu Huraira (radi allahu anhu) narrated that the Messenger of Allah ﷺ said:

"Al Haya is from faith, and faith is in Paradise. Obscenity is from rudeness and rudeness is in the fire."

(Jami at-Tirmidhi)

A person who uses obscene language and curses often, has lost haya of their tongue. Those who sin openly and act haughty, rude and disrespectful, have lost haya of their character and those who dress provocatively and reveal their awrah, have lost haya over their body.

If we feel no guilt whilst doing any of the above, then each of us should really worry about the state of our Imaan and the state of our heart.

Ibn Umar (radi Allahu anhuma) said,

"Modesty and belief are together. If one of them is removed, the other is removed."

(Al-Adab Al-Mufrad)

Inner modesty is very important for us, as believers. It is what shapes us and keeps us steadfast and grounded.

However along with inner modesty, also comes outer modesty which is just as important.

Both are related to each other and are included in our Hijab.

What is Hijab?

Hijab means to conceal or cover, and it refers to the dress code required for Muslim women to observe when they step out of their homes or are in the presence of non mahram men. This legislation is fardh (compulsory) upon every believing woman once she hits puberty.

Contrary to popular opinion however, Hijab does not mean just a head covering. Rather it is the covering of the entire body except the hands, face and the feet (according to the Hanafi madhab. The other madhahib [schools of thought within fiqh] say feet should be covered too).

Men also have a hijab, but for them it refers to covering everything from between their naval and their knees.

Also it is important to note that the hijab encompasses much more than the outer wear and appearance of a believer; it also includes the mannerisms, attitude and behaviour of a Muslim too.

We shall however focus on the Hijab for women because it is what has been specifically stated for us in the Holy Qur'an. My beloved sister, the Hijab is a commandment from Allah ﷻ, and He Honours us by informing us of that which is pleasing to Him.

Allah ﷻ says in the Holy Qur'an:

"O Prophet, tell your wives and your daughters and the women of the believers to bring down over themselves [part] of their outer garments. That is more suitable that they will be known and not be abused. And ever is Allah Forgiving and Merciful."

(Surah Al-Ahzab, 59)

The verses of Hijab were revealed at a time when the mushrikeen of Makkah would tease Muslim women and would use the excuse that they could not tell that they were Muslim. Allah sent these verses so as to differentiate the believing women from the disbelieving women and from the slave girls. This would leave the mushrikeen, hypocrites and wrong doers no excuse to flirt with women who had been honoured by Islam.

When the verses of covering were revealed, the women at the time rushed to cover themselves up in their eagerness to observe and comply with Allah's commands. Some even ripped their curtains and shrouded themselves in it because they found no other form of covering. They embraced the Hijab with zeal and without a moments hesitation and recognised the benefits it would bring them. They were eager to hear and obey, whilst today we tend to hear and delay.

It is a ruling and a dress code designed to protect females from sexual advances from predatory men and to minimise moral degradation in society, but most importantly it is a commandment from Allah. It has many benefits when acted upon properly, as all of Allah's commandments do. It shields women from perverted stares, superficial scrutiny and the sexual exploitation of women based on their looks. It is true that there are some extremely perverted men who make sexual advances and have fetishes of even Hijabi women, however the Hijab helps reduce the general exploitation of women in society.

An added benefit to the woman who observes the Hijab, is the fact that it is a constant reminder that we are Muslim women and so are bound by certain rules and a code of conduct. When we step out of our homes shaytaan tempts us to sin and to go towards places of sin, however when observed correctly the Hijab acts as a barrier and a reminder for us. It shields us from our own temptations and desires and helps keep us grounded and focused on our duties as a muslimah.

A believing woman is a woman who strives to please Allah and does not encourage or enjoy the stares or attention of strange men. Hijab is a literal God sent blessing for us, and when we realise that we begin to see its beauty and benefit in our daily lives.

The struggles we face today when observing it are the same struggles that the first believing women faced, and so we can take courage from examples of their courage and lessons from their steadfastness and approach towards the Hijab. It was strange in their time, and it is considered strange and oppressive in the eyes of many today. In a world where a females value is often placed upon how attractive she is and so much emphasis is placed on her outer beauty, her internal beauty and character count for very little.

Islam however teaches that a woman is to be respected for her virtuous character and mannerisms rather than her external looks which do not count towards who she is as a person. In a society where a woman is first judged on how attractive she is, the

Hijab diverts the attention from the outer and forces people to recognise and pay attention to her character, piety and intellect.

It is empowering and a powerful display of a strong woman who is independent of the need to impress others.

"My value as a woman is not measured by the size of my waist or the number of men who like me. My worth as a human being is measured on a higher scale: a scale of righteousness and piety. And my purpose in life-despite what fashion magazines say-is something more sublime than just looking good for men."

— Yasmin Mogahed, Reclaim Your Heart

It is an important act of obedience and worship for the Muslim woman. If you have yet to taste the sweetness of obeying this beautiful commandment of Allah ﷻ, I encourage you to learn about it and embrace it.

Dearest sister, take it a step at a time if you need to, but do not waste time in just planning to wear it and not actually getting around to observing this fardh. Life is never guaranteed, and death can come to us at any time, so please do not delay. It is never too late to start, so start by making the intention to do so. If anything, you will still be rewarded for your intention and if your intentions are sincere Allah ﷻ will make it easy for you. May Allah ﷻ make it easy for us all.

Ignore the comments of those who mock the Hijab and claim it is the epitome of regression and backward thinking. They do not understand the sense of freedom the Hijab instils in the heart of the covered woman. It is oppressive in the eyes of everyone, except the woman wearing it who accepts it with her whole heart.

Do not listen to those who say you have to be "perfect" in order to start covering. This is nonsense. Every single human is flawed and all believers are sinners. The only difference is that we wish to be amongst those sinners who repent and strive to be better and excel as much as we can in our Deen. If it is something that Allah has decreed for us, it is our duty to accept and obey.

I quote the Hijabi nobel peace prize winner and human rights activist, Tawakkol Karman, who said beautifully,

> *"Man in early times was almost naked, and as his intellect evolved he started wearing clothes. What I am today and what I'm wearing represents the highest level of thought and civilization that man has achieved, and is not regressive. It's the removal of clothes again that is a regression back to the ancient times."*

It is important to mention the conditions that need to be understood and fulfilled to correctly observe the Hijab. It is only when these conditions are met, that our Hijab will be considered correct.

Conditions of Hijab

It must cover the whole body except the hands and face and should be loose and not clinging to your form. The curves of a female's body should not be on display and the covering should not be of a thin see-through fabric either. Tight jeans and trousers, tight jersey dresses and skirts, see-through tops which expose the colour and shape of body and undergarments; these are all impermissible.

Abu Hurayra radi allahu anhu said,

> *"Women who are naked even though they are wearing clothes, go astray and make others go astray, and they will not enter the Garden and they will not find it's scent, and it's scent is experienced from as far as the*

distance travelled in five hundred years."

(Muwatta Imam Malik)

"Women who are naked even though they are wearing clothes" refers to tight form fitting clothing, and sheer clothing that shows the colour of skin.

"Go astray and make others go astray", because once you feel no shame in wearing revealing clothing, you will start to become accustomed to dressing in that manner. This can corrupt the hearts of those who see you, and can influence other sisters to copy you.

"They will not enter the Garden and they will not find it's scent." This is such a grave consequence of not observing the hijab correctly. May Allah protect us all.

This however, does not mean that you can never enter Jannah, if you dress in a revealing manner. For Allah is The Most Just and Most Forgiving. Turn to Him in repentance, ask for His guidance and start covering for His Sake.

Spraying perfume on yourself and your clothes when you are going out in a space where non mahram men will be able to smell your scent is also against the rulings of Hijab. Perfume attracts and invites attention and so should be avoided in the presence of non mahrams. If however, you are amongst women and at home, then perfume yourself with all the best perfumes that you like and look good for yourself and your family in sha Allah.

Islam is not oppressive my lovely sister, there is just a balance that we need to respect. We are allowed to enjoy the comforts of dressing nicely and doing our hair up, wearing make-up and perfume and beautifying ourselves. It is actually encouraged to look beautiful for ourselves, our family and husband and we receive good deeds for looking after ourselves. Islam just asks that we keep it to our homes and then cover when we go outside.

So all in all, for our Hijab to be considered correct it should be loose, the whole body should be covered without our body shape or skin showing, it should not be clingy or sheer and it should not be perfumed.

We can wear loose baggy trousers with long loose tops, and loose full length maxi dresses- these are all fine and fit in with the requirements of Shari'ah.

It is so important to mention the correct Hijab, not to point fingers at anyone who might not observe it 100% correctly, but rather to encourage any sister reading this to take the next steps towards covering a little more.

As long as you know what is required and accept what is considered correct and incorrect, then even if you are struggling and do not observe it properly as of yet, you will continue trying to better yourself. It is only when we become complacent and make excuses for where we slip up that it causes problems. We will never improve, if we are going to constantly make excuses for ourselves.

My dear sister, Shaytaan does not want the best for us. He is patient and takes his time hoping to misguide us. He uses all his efforts to take us further and further away from what Allah ﷻ wants and has decreed for us.

One of his tricks is to slowly ease us into uncovering more and more. He does this a step at a time, normalising each stage for us until we do not realise that we have given more and more of our Hijab up. It starts with our clothing becoming tighter and shorter and the scarf on our head slipping further and further back.

I went abroad to study the Deen in 2005. At that time, in my community it was not common for Muslim sisters to wear tight leggings or jeans. Only a few would wear really tight leggings, and they were sisters who usually did not observe the hijab. When I came back to the UK 8 years later however, I was surprised to see almost every sister wore skinny jeans and leggings. Some wore tights and short skirts, which before would have been unheard of. Now it has gradually become even worse, with sisters uncovering their neck, legs and arms. It is a world wide problem.

The reason for mentioning this is not to judge these sisters, but rather to raise the issue that with time we are losing more and more of our Islamic code of dress without even realising it. It is so crucial that we realise this and reflect on ourselves and work to improve.

The Hijab is being abused. We have become lazy in our attitude towards this beautiful fardh, and have lost the true understanding of it.

Social media influencers who start off observing the Hijab correctly, have slowly found ways to beautify it and style it in ways that are not acceptable for it to be considered Hijab. Younger sisters are watching these sisters and becoming influenced to wear their scarves in the same way and to dress in a similar style. Watering down a fardh in our Deen, to the point that it has become just a fashion statement for many is an evil that is becoming more and more widespread.

Hijabi Instagram bloggers and YouTubers are struggling themselves and that is completely understandable. But following their ways of dressing and believing it to be fine is not correct. They become a role model even if they do not want to be and this creates a generation of younger girls who want to look like them and implement their styles in the way they dress. This is evident in the amount of sisters who have begun to wear "turban" hijab styles and have their front fringe and neck showing. Hair that is meticulously styled flows out from our scarf as our head coverings slip further and further back.

Arms and lower legs are bared now and every inch of our bodies are visible with all our curves on show.

The more we allow ourselves to dress in this manner without feeling guilt, the worse our covering will become. I write this with a lot of love for all of my sisters, as I do understand and experience the difficulties we face. We have become so comfortable in trying to look "good" and trying to follow the fashions of today that we have willingly given more and more of our modesty up in the process. We unfortunately are failing the Hijab and are abusing and causing great injustice to the meaning of it.

My lovely sister who is struggling with her Hijab but observing it correctly, I congratulate you, because as long as you struggle and stay firm Allah ﷻ will help you and make your affairs easier for you. You will gain rewards for every moment of your struggle making it very much worth it.

My dear sister who is struggling and has stumbled in the process, allowing her hijab to slip in some way or form; You are stronger than you feel you are and I send you love and support.

As long as you have breath in your body, you always have time to improve. We all do. Make the intention to strive harder and do not allow yourself to fail. I know it is much easier said than done but I promise you it can be done. You can climb those steps towards the correct form of covering again.

I am proud of you. You are covering and trying for the sake of Allah in a most difficult testing time and I pray Allah makes it easy for you and for us all.

Our tests in our life are our own, and it is up to us to keep ourselves on the path of the righteous. We can only attain that path by pushing ourselves to do good, and by correctly observing the mandatory actions that Allah ﷻ has ordained for us to the best of our ability. Subhan Allah, day in and out, we wear the Hijab and face the mocking and abuse of those who are ignorant to the concept of covering. We struggle so much and face so much discrimination. Wouldn't we want all that struggle to mean something? How would we feel if we worked hard all day but our work was faulty and we did not gain any fruits from our labour?

The same can be said about Hijab. Our struggles are valid and seen by Allah, but why diminish the rewards we could be receiving because we did not observe it correctly. I encourage you all to take the first few steps towards perfecting your Hijab, and as long as you are actively working towards improving, you are doing well.

I am not suggesting throw out all your clothes and buy a whole new wardrobe of only jilbabs and jubbahs, but rather start by wearing longer tops when going out and looser clothing. Cover your hair fully and tuck away the fringe. Swap the tight jeans for baggy trousers or skirts. Have fabric added to your dresses to make them longer or go for clothing that is fully lined and loose rather than sheer and skin-tight. Wear sleeves with sleeveless dresses and swap your perfume for body-spray.

Just take it a step at a time my dear sister. Take it at your own pace. Work towards improving and building upon each step and in sha Allah before long you will ease yourself into loose clothing, jilbabs and more appropriate Islamic dress.

The deeds that are small but consistent are most pleasing to Allah. Remember that Hijab is an outward display of your devotion and love for Him. Wear it with pride and in a manner that is pleasing to the One who ordained it upon you.

My dear sister, the beauty about Islam is that we can always improve. Always. Every single one of us can find ways to go that one step further and do more than we were doing the day before. Lets embrace change and push ourselves further. The more we challenge ourselves, the more progress we can make. May Allah

﷽ purify our intentions and make it easy for us all. With the Help of Allah ﷻ, we've got this!

My veil gives me strength and purpose and is my choice to display my faith proudly. When you look at me you do not see just any woman, you see a Muslim woman who is not ashamed or afraid of being who she truly is. My sights are set higher. Rather than be judged for how I look by the creation, I choose to be judged by My Creator for my faith.

This is my armour that I wear with pride and dignity. I do not strive to be noticed by strange men nor do I need their predatory gaze to feel like more of a woman. They say my Hijab forces me into invisibility. Yet I say my veil forces you to acknowledge that I am a woman who needs not bare her body in order to be seen.

This wasn't always the case and wasn't always how I felt. I wore the hijab since I was very young so it was like second nature to me, however I started wearing the niqab when I was still in high school and so went through a period of time when I was bullied because of it. This made it very difficult for me and at one stage I did not want to wear it anymore. I lost the excitement I had felt when I first observed it.

With time, deep reflection and a period of taking it off and putting it back on, I finally decided to just push away the negative thoughts and fears I had and I started to wear it again. I prayed to Allah that He would grant me the confidence and the will to observe it correctly, and Allah accepted my supplications, making it much easier the second time around.

Many sisters do have valid concerns about having to deal with Islamophobes and Islamophobic remarks, and this can make observing the hijab seem quite daunting.

My advice would be to just keep your trust in Allah and take the leap. Sometimes we think of something to be much more daunting than it actually is. You may find it difficult at first but mostly there aren't any issues and it grows easier to observe with time.

We all go through different phases and some days it can be more difficult than others. It's up to us to remind ourselves on them days about why we observe the hijab and what benefits are gained from doing so correctly.

Wear your Hijab with your head held high my sister. Surrounded by nakedness, the more you cover, the more empowered you will feel.

"How beautiful to remain a mystery in a world of people who have nothing left to hide."

True beauty is found within the heart, not on the face. Why waste so much time trying to look beautiful when outward beauty is so short-lived. The more we find comfort in worship, the more we will realise that the garments of piety make us truly the most beautiful women in the world.

"In essence, if we want to direct our lives, we must take control of our consistent actions. It's not what we do once in a while that shapes our lives, but what we do consistently."

*

"A little progress everyday adds up to big results."

PART 2

BENEFICIAL KNOWLEDGE

CHAPTER 4

From the cradle to the grave

It was narrated from Jabir that: the Messenger of Allah ﷺ said:

"Ask Allah for beneficial knowledge and seek refuge with Allah from knowledge that is of no benefit."

(Sunan ibn Majah)

Seeking knowledge is so important for every male and female. We are liable for our deeds and so are required to seek the knowledge we need, in order to commit to our worship and fulfil our duties.

Allah ﷻ says in the Holy Qur'an,

"Say, "Are those who know equal to those who do not know?"

(Surah Az-Zumar, verse 9)

In other words, they are not equal, just as the person of knowledge is not equal to the ignorant one.

In another verse Allah ﷻ says:

"Only those fear Allah from among His servants who have knowledge. Indeed, Allah is Exalted in Might and Forgiving."

(Surah Fatir, verse 28)

When a person is unaware of the attributes of Allah ﷻ they will be fearless of Him. However the more a person is aware and has knowledge of His attributes and Powers, His Knowledge, His

Wrath, Wisdom and His Omnipotence, the more he/she will be fearful and in awe of Him ﷺ. The one who is fearless of God is illiterate even if he/she has all the knowledge of the world. And the one who knows the attributes of God and fears Him in their heart, is learned even if he/she is illiterate.

True knowledge makes one afraid, as our true purpose in this life is made clearer, our responsibilities increase and so does our level of consciousness of Allah. We no longer look at sins as big or little sins but rather we have a realisation of The One in Whose presence the sins are being committing.

Along with fear we also need to have hope and good expectations with Allah. For He is Merciful and Forgiving and it is necessary that we balance both our fear of Him and our Hope in Him. We learn about both and without this education we would fail in our worship of Him.

Zaid b. Alqam reported:

I am not going to say anything but only that which Allah's Messenger (may peace be upon him) used to say. He used to supplicate;

" O Allah, I seek refuge in Thee from incapacity, from sloth, from cowardice, from miserliness, decrepitude and from torment of the grave. O Allah, grant to my soul the sense of righteousness and purify it, for Thou art the Best Purifier thereof. Thou art the Protecting Friend thereof, and Guardian thereof. O Allah, I seek refuge in Thee from the knowledge which does not benefit, from the heart that does not entertain the fear (of Allah), from the soul that does not feel contented and the supplication that is not responded."

(Sahih Muslim)

The more knowledge a person has, the more it should humble them and draw them closer to Allah ﷻ.

This is incumbent upon every believer, as we all worship him and seek to grow closer to Him ﷻ.

Anas ibn Malik narrated that the Prophet ﷺ said:

"Seeking knowledge is obligatory for every Muslim, male and female."

[Ibn Maajah]

It is an obligation upon us and so should not be treated lightly. Our primary concern should be that of learning our religion. This includes the many branches of knowledge connected to understanding our Deen. A few of which are; Hifdh (memorising the Qur'an) Tafseer (understanding the Holy Qur'an), Fiqh (islamic jurisprudence), Hadith studies, Aqeedah (creed) etc.

This is the most important and most beneficial knowledge of all.

To delve into the waters of our religion, is to sip on the chalice of truth. There is so much to learn and the scholars have spent their lives in pursuit of it; yet they feel that they haven't even touched the surface.

This knowledge brings us closer to Allah ﷻ, for indeed how can you worship your Creator when you have no knowledge of Him. Learning of Him makes us Love and Fear Him as He ought to be Loved and Feared. We learn of His Mercy and His Wrath and this helps us obey Him and fulfil our true purpose. Having Knowledge of The Almighty, helps us improve our quality of worship, and satisfies the cravings of our soul.

My lovely sister, we have already mentioned some female companions of the Messenger of Allah ﷺ, who were scholars and teachers and spent their life in pursuit of learning and imparting the knowledge they gained upon others.

In Islam women have always been encouraged to spread their wings and delve into the pursuit of 'ilm.

Education is seen as a pivotal factor in determining the social, economic and political advancements in society. How can a society be deemed as advanced if fifty percent of the people are uneducated.

Unfortunately in many parts of the Muslim world women are denied this basic fundamental need and right for fair education and it leads to injustice and to women being treated secondary to men.

This is an extremely damaging, sad reflection of Muslim societies and it is against the Sunnah of the Messenger of Allah ﷺ and against the teachings of the Deen.

A study into the life of The Prophet ﷺ shows that he made special arrangements for women and encouraged their desire to learn more.

Narrated by Abu Sa`id Al-Khudri:

Some women requested the Prophet ﷺ to fix a day for them as the men were taking all his time. On that he promised them one day for religious lessons and commandments.

Once during such a lesson the Prophet ﷺ said, "A woman whose three children die will be shielded by them from the Hell fire." On that a woman asked, "If only two die?" He replied, "Even two (will shield her from the

Hell-fire).

(Sahih al Bukhari)

This hadith clearly demonstrates the attitude the Messenger of Allah ﷺ had towards women seeking knowledge. He did not admonish them or forbid them, rather he allotted a separate class just for them upon their request.

It was only in the 19th century that higher education began to blossom for women in the west and around the world. Prior to this, only a few women gained access to education and most of them had to become nuns and had to enter the convent in order to do so. Women had to fight for their right to be educated and taken seriously and the few who did were the exception. Even they had to change themselves in some way to be accepted into the circles of knowledge, such as Plato's student Lastheneia who had to attend classes dressed as a man. Coloured women weren't allowed to attend till much later in the west and younger women were also barred from classes.

Yet 1400 years ago Muslim women were scholars, led their own classes and were held in high esteem. Slaves and free women alike, young and old, all were included in this and none were exempt.

In the Holy Qur'an and ahadith wherever the importance of knowledge has been expressed, it has been expressed for both genders and there has been no exception or preference given to men in this regard.

Abud-Darda (May Allah be pleased with him) reported: The Messenger of Allah ﷺ said,

"He who follows a path in quest of knowledge, Allah will make the path of Jannah easy to him.

The angels lower their wings over the seeker of knowledge, being pleased with what he does. The inhabitants of the heavens and the earth and even the fish in the depth of the oceans seek forgiveness for him. The superiority of the learned man over the devout worshipper is like that of the full moon to the rest of the stars (i.e., in brightness). The learned are the heirs of the Prophets who bequeath neither dinar nor dirham but only that of knowledge; and he who acquires it, has in fact acquired an abundant portion."

(Abu Dawood and At-Tirmidhi)

Education is a matter of religious duty and leads to the understanding of the concept of submission to The Creator and to a deeper understanding of Him.

Allah ﷻ gave Adam alayhi slaam higher status than all of the angels, due to the fact that He granted him knowledge of the names of all things.

"And He taught Adam the names - all of them. Then He showed them to the angels and said, "Inform Me of the names of these, if you are truthful."

"They said, "Exalted are You; we have no knowledge except what You have taught us. Indeed, it is You who is the Knowing, the Wise."

"He said, "O Adam, inform them of their names." And when he had informed them of their names, He said, "Did I not tell you that I know the unseen [aspects] of the heavens and the earth? And I know what you reveal and what you have concealed."

(Surah Al- Baqarah, verses 31, 32 and 33)

Along with religious sciences, worldly sciences are also a necessity and a need. Particularly in the medical and nursing factions as it's best for women to go to a woman for health reasons and the like.

Indeed our mother A'isha Radi Allaha anha was learned in medicine and healing and she grew experienced in this when she had to look after the Messenger of Allah ﷺ during his illness in his last days. Other women from amongst the companions were trained nurses and often tended to the wounded on the battlefield.

That being said, it is not just medicine or nursing we should venture into. Rather all knowledge is good and praise worthy if it is of practical use and a benefit to the society we live in.

Sufyaan Ibn Uyainah said:

"If knowledge does not benefit you it will harm you"

The aim is to excel in education so we can benefit ourselves, our children, and benefit society as a whole. If our intentions are sincere and we set out to seek knowledge for the sake of Allah then it is considered worship. However if we seek it in order to have pride, to show off or to argue with those with little knowledge, then we will gain only sin and no benefit.

In recent times it has become extremely easy to attain knowledge. We have easy access to books, the wide web at our fingertips and many many recordings and resources which help us learn. There is no longer any excuse not to study as we can even learn from the comfort of our homes without having to go out of the house.

Muslim women are often viewed as taking a back seat and

contributing little to the spread of the Deen. But, this is far from the reality.

Often their achievements have been overshadowed by their male counterparts, however they have made significant contributions. They have issued their own fatawa (islamic rulings derived from text) wrote books, and even been teachers of some of the most well known and celebrated male scholars.

A few notable female scholars after the Sahabiyat:

Amrah Bint Abdur Rahman

From amongst these women we have the likes of Amrah bint Abdur Rahman. She was from the generation that came after that of the companions of the prophet ﷺ.

She was a jurist, a scholar, and a specialist in ahadith. The great Caliph Umar bin 'Abdul 'Aziz used to say:

"If you want to learn ahadith go to Amrah."

She taught some of the greatest scholars and they would flock to her lessons to soak up her vast knowledge of Hadith. She was so well known for her high level of 'ilm that if she gave a ruling on a matter, it was never questioned, it was accepted and acted upon straight away.

Imam Zuhri used to say:

"Go to Amrah, she is a vast vessel of hadith."

Umm Darda

Umm Darda is a very notable name in the circles of Islamic knowledge. She taught in Damascus and in Jerusalem. Her classes were attended by Imams, Jurists, and hadith scholars in huge numbers.

She taught for the majority of her life and in her old age, she was served by some of her students, who helped her return to her place of teaching after the prayer.

Fatimah bint Ibrahim b. Jowhar

Fatimah bint Ibrahim was a very famous teacher of Imam Bukhari. She lived around the beginning of the eighth century of the Muslim calendar.

Great Imams, the likes of Subqi and Dhahabi studied the whole of Sahih Bukhari under her.

She taught in the mosque of the Messenger of Allah ﷺ in Madinah, and would lean against his grave as she taught in her old age.

She was so well known that people flocked to attend her classes and anticipated her visit to their mosques.

Ayesha bint Abdul Hadi

This great scholar taught in the grand mosque of Damascus and was appointed by the Sultan of the time as the Master of Hadith. She taught the compilation of Sahih Bukhari and there was no one in her community who could compare to her scholarly authority.

Imam Ibn Hajar Al-Asqalani studied more than 100 books with her.

Her chain of narration in hadith is considered strong and sound and between her and Imam Bukhari are eight transmitters.

She played a major role in preserving and accurately conveying ahadith.

Women have played a vital role in helping preserve our Deen and helping spread the correct teachings found within, and continue to do so. Reading and learning about their contributions brings a smile to my face and pleases my heart. They may not be commonly known today, but we reap the benefits of their efforts to spread the Deen and their reward is with Allah.

Dear sister, the ummah needs women of knowledge at all times. Women are the backbone of society as they raise the generations to come and an intelligent scholarly mother will raise children who in turn will excel in knowledge and provide much benefit to her community.

Abu Hurairah (May Allah be pleased with him) reported:
The Messenger of Allah ﷺ said,

"The world, with all that it contains, is accursed except for the remembrance of Allah that which pleases Allah; and the religious scholars and seekers of knowledge."

(At-Tirmidhi)

We can spend our whole life in the pursuit of attaining knowledge and yet there will always be much more to learn. The human mind is a wondrous thing but we can only learn that which Allah has made clear to us.

The more we learn the more we realise we do not know. I urge you sister, please take the first steps towards seeking knowledge and fight for your right to do so. This is the right of every human, male or female, young or old. It is a necessity and a means to knowing your Creator and understanding our Deen.

The great scholars of the past, the likes of Imam Shafi'I and

Imam Maalik were encouraged upon the path of knowledge by their righteous mothers. Their mothers pushed them towards studying the Deen and spent much upon their studies.

Great mothers produce great children and when a mother is focused on a goal, she can encourage her children towards that goal.

Make use of the resources you have around you and I challenge you to take up a new subject to study.

May Allah open the doors of knowledge for you and allow you to act upon that which you learn. For what is knowledge without amal.

"Knowledge without action is like a tree without fruit."

Scholars and their sacrifices in the path of knowledge

Ibn Aqīl said,
"I try my very best to limit the time I spend eating, to such an extent that I choose dry biscuit and a sip of water over eating bread, because of the difference in chewing [time] between the two, so as to save my time for reading or writing down some useful ideas.
The best thing for the wise man to save is time."

.

Abū Dāwūd as-Sijistānī used to tailor one sleeve of his garment wider than the other. When he was asked about it he said, "The wider sleeve is for books and the other is not in need of it.

Muhammad ibn Yūnus said,

"I wrote hadīth in al-Basrāh from one thousand, one hundred and eighty-six men."

.

Ibn al-Qāsim said,
"Seeking knowledge caused Malik ibn Anas to demolish the roof of his house and sell it's wood."

.

Abdulrahman bin Abi Hatem said:

"We were in Egypt for seven months and we did not eat broth, our day was split for gathering with scholars, and in the evening for copying (writing down) and meetings. So one day I was with an elderly companion of mine and it was said to me that he is sick, so on our way we saw a nice fish and we bought it. When we arrived home, the time for the gathering (of knowledge) arrived, so we did not have time to prepare it and we headed towards the gathering. We continued in this manner until three days had passed and the fish had changed so we ate it raw because we did not even have time to have it fried.

Knowledge is not attained with comfort of the body"

The righteous scholars who have benefited and spread the teachings of Islam acquired that knowledge through immense personal physical sacrifices and spent every moment they could learning what they could. They spent in the way of knowledge and gained more as a result.

The path of knowledge is not easy, but it is a path of worship and clarity.

My dear sister, let us take a step on this path and dip our feet into the cool waters of the ocean of knowledge in front of us. May it be a means of gaining Allah's pleasure.

"The pursuit of knowledge is never-ending

The day you stop seeking knowledge is the day you stop growing."

PART 3

THE SECRET OF TRUE HAPPINESS

CHAPTER 5

To be the happiest woman alive is to know that Allah Loves You

My dearest sister, every single human being is in a search to find true happiness. Some look for it in wealth, others in material objects, whilst a believer finds joy in pleasing Allah.

The wealthiest of men chase material gain and drown themselves in riches, yet the accumulation of their mansions, sports cars and designer clothing does not result in true happiness. They often become the most miserable of people, committing suicide and turning towards drugs as an escape.

However those who do that which Allah Commands, and avoid that which He Forbids, they have a light from Allah and no one is happier than them.

Allah promises them a good, content life:

"Whoever does righteousness, whether male or female, while he is a believer - We will surely cause him to live a good life, and We will surely give them their reward [in the Hereafter] according to the best of what they used to do."

(Surah-An-Nahl, verse 97)

By His Generosity, He does not let down the ones who put their hope in Him, and He does not neglect the Ones who love Him.

Is it not a huge blessing from Allah ﷻ that He guided us and made us amongst the believers and from the Ummah of the last Messenger, Muhammad ﷺ

This alone is a sign of His love for us, as He guides whom He wills and whomever He wants goodness for.

He ﷻ has granted us faith and through our faith we are blessed with strength and tranquillity, unlike anything else this world can give us.

The "restrictions" and "dos and do nots" that have been legislated for us can seem extreme and harsh to some, but really they are a means for us to achieve self control and become more aware of our actions.

Our true purpose is to worship Allah ﷻ and glorify Him and the aim is to live our lives in ways that Allah ﷻ loves, in order to gain His love.

We forget how short this worldly life is and we busy ourselves in Dunya matters. If only we realised just how insignificant this world is, whilst remembering how important our deeds in this life are, for they determine our place in the Hereafter.

Allah ﷻ has gifted us five daily prayers to gently remind us throughout our day of our true purpose. He has granted us these short breaks in our routine to work on the state of our heart. This is an example of how He ﷻ looks after His Creation. He ensures we do not neglect the state of our souls whilst we busy ourselves in providing for our families, and so He has made prayer compulsory upon us and distributed it perfectly with different timings throughout the day and night. This makes it easy for us to continuously turn back to Him and redirect our thoughts and hearts towards Him.

We worry about having food on the table to nourish our bodies, so He provides us with our daily rizq (provision) but also with food for our souls in the form of prayer. He looks after and cares for our outer and our inner condition.

He has blessed us with Ramadhan, a month of fasting, so we can have one month dedicated to reconnecting and refocusing our attention towards our Deen.

These are ways that Allah ﷻ shows us His love for us. Gentle reminders.

Sometimes He ﷻ places hardship on our paths in order to forgive our sins and make it easy for us to gain good deeds. Many of us become heedless in times of ease and forget our true purpose and by placing hardship in our way, Allah ﷻ is redirecting our attention towards worship, sabr (patience) and gratitude. This is from His Mercy and love for His slaves, although few understand.

Waki' bin Hudus narrated that his paternal uncle Abu Razin said:

"The Messenger of Allah said: 'Allah laughs at the despair of His slaves although He soon changes it.' I said: 'O Messenger of Allah, does the Lord laugh?' He said: 'Yes.' I said: 'We shall never be deprived of good by a Lord Who laughs.'"

(Sunan Ibn Majah)

Allah ﷻ laughs in a manner befitting His Majesty, and He ﷻ does so because He ﷻ Knows that relief is around the corner for His slaves. He ﷻ Knows what we do not know and Sees what we do not see. His Knowledge and Power encompasses all, and He promises that after every hardship there is ease.

Our aim in life is to gain His pleasure, and we do so by living our life according to the carefully transmitted order of our Deen.

We use our life in this Dunya to prepare for the Hereafter, and to gain eternal bliss in Jannah (Paradise); this is our ultimate goal.

Sahl bin Sa'd As-Sa'idi (May Allah be pleased with him) reported:

A man came to the Prophet ﷺ and said, "O Messenger of Allah, guide me to such an action which, if I do Allah

will love me and the people will also love me." He ﷺ
*said, "Have no desire for this world, Allah will love
you; and have no desire for what people possess, and the
people will love you."*

[Ibn Majah]

Dear sister, at times life can be difficult and fraught with hardship, and other times it can be wonderful and full of happiness and joy. This is our test.

Allah ﷻ says in the Holy Quran,

"And We will surely test you with something of fear and hunger and a loss of wealth and lives and fruits, but give good tidings to the patient,"

(surah al Baqarah, verse 155)

And Who are the patient ones? In the following verse He says;
"Who, when disaster strikes them, say, "Indeed we belong to Allah, and indeed to Him we will return."

Those are the ones upon whom are blessings from their Lord and mercy. And it is those who are the [rightly] guided.

(Surah Al Baqarah, Verses 156 and 157)

So how do we pull through and keep ourselves firm upon the Deen, and ensure we pass this test? The ayaat (verse of Qur'an) mentioned above are beautiful pointers on how we can benefit from our hardships by turning to Allah in our times of need and having patience especially at the first strike of loss. This includes thinking well of Allah and reminding yourself that the difficulty you are facing shall pass.

It is from Allah's Mercy upon us that He has granted us The Messenger of Allah ﷺ, and through his seerah (his life and example) and carefully transmitted and preserved ahadith, we are blessed with countless lessons and examples of how to behave, what mindset to carry, and how to deal with the good and bad that befalls us.

There are several ahadith that mention the rewards of turning to Allah in times of difficulty, admitting that ultimately everything belongs to and returns to Him ﷻ.

These ahadith teach us how to ask Him ﷻ for Help.

Umm Salamah (May Allah be pleased with her) reported: I heard the Messenger of Allah ﷺ saying,

"When a person suffers from a calamity and utters:

'Inna lillahi wa inna ilaihi raji'un. Allahumma ujurni fi musibati, wakhluf li khairan minha

(We belong to Allah and to Him we shall return. O Allah! Compensate me in my affliction, recompense my loss and give me something better in exchange for it), then Allah surely compensates him with reward and better substitute."

Umm Salamah (May Allah be pleased with her) said:

When Abu Salamah (May Allah be pleased with him) died, I repeated the same supplication as the Messenger of Allah ﷺ had commanded me (to do). So Allah bestowed upon me a better substitute than him (I was married to Muhammad, the Messenger of Allah ﷺ.

Ask Allah ﷻ to grant you ease and He will reward you with better than what you have lost and will fill your heart with the tranquillity you seek.

There are levels to this my sister. The salaf (pious predecessors) and great scholars have the understanding that every state a believer is in is a beautiful state for him/her. They have the understanding that a calamity that makes you turn to Allah is better for you than a blessing which makes you forget the remembrance of Allah.

The Messenger of Allah ﷺ said,

"How wonderful is the case of a believer; there is good for him in everything and this applies only to a believer. If prosperity attends him, he expresses gratitude to Allah and that is good for him; and if adversity befalls him, he endures it patiently and that is better for him"

(Sahih Muslim)

Islamic tradition teaches us to pray, supplicate, learn about our Deen and act upon that which we learn. Also to make sure we're vigorous in upholding our fara'idh (obligatory actions) and beautify our ibadah with the sunnan and nawafil.

Raise families upon the way of the pious predecessors and instil the love of the Deen, and the love of Allah ﷻ and His Messengers in our young.

We must carry ourselves with integrity and honour and in a manner befitting a believing woman. Always check and re-check our intentions and always strive to gain the pleasure of Allah.

Be patient with the trials that befall us, and remind ourselves that we all belong to Allah ﷻ and to Him we shall return.

This is how we pass our test and gain The Mercy and Favour of Allah!

Abud-Darda' (May Allah be pleased with him) reported:

The Messenger of Allah ﷺ said, "One of Prophet Dawud's supplications was: 'Allahumma inni as'aluka hubbaka, wa hubba man yuhibbuka, wal-'amalalladhi yuballighuni hubbaka. Allahumm-aj'al hubbaka ahabba ilayya min nafsi, wa ahli, wa minal-ma'il-baridi

(O Allah! I ask You for Your Love, the love of those who love You, and deeds which will cause me to attain Your Love. O Allah! Make Your Love dearer to me than myself, my family and the cold water).'"

[At- Tirmidhi].

Like a traveller craves cold water in the desert, and would give anything for a single sip, that is how dear the love of Allah ﷺ should be for us. No, it should be even dearer than that.

Dearer to us than ourselves and everything we hold precious.

It is the reason behind our very existence. Without the love of Allah, there is no real meaning of existence.

We submit to Allah ﷺ and work to gain His favour. We haven't been left to wander and find the answers without any guidance. Allah ﷺ has sent us Prophets and Messengers throughout time, and blessed us with the Last and final Messenger ﷺ, to guide us towards the true path.

Allah ﷺ says in the Holy Qur'an,

"Say, [O Muhammad], "If you should love Allah, then follow me, [so] Allah will love you and forgive you your

sins. And Allah is Forgiving and Merciful." (Surah Ale-'Imran, 3:31)

So to gain success in this life and the Hereafter, we need to act upon the commandments of Allah. Everything that has been made compulsory upon us, is for our own benefit, and a means to grow closer to Him ﷻ.

My beloved sister, this life is so short and yet we get so caught up in it. If we commit to the few obligations upon us, we will be setting ourselves up for an everlasting life of bliss in the Hereafter, bi idh'nillah.

Abu Hurairah (May Allah be pleased with him) reported: Messenger of Allah ﷺ said,

"Allah the Exalted has said: 'I will declare war against him who shows hostility to a pious worshipper of Mine. And the most beloved thing with which My slave comes nearer to Me is what I have enjoined upon him; and My slave keeps on coming closer to Me through performing Nawafil (prayer or doing extra deeds besides what is obligatory) till I love him. When I love him I become his hearing with which he hears, his seeing with which he sees, his hand with which he strikes, and his leg with which he walks; and if he asks (something) from Me, I give him, and if he asks My Protection (refuge), I protect him".

[Al- Bukhari].

The more we walk upon this path of true Love, the more Allah ﷻ will make our journey easy for us. When we are concious of Him in our affairs, He helps us in ways we can not even possibly imagine.

His Love for us knows no bounds. When He ﷻ loves us, He orders the angels and then the pious to love us.

Narrated by Abu Huraira:

The Prophet ﷺ said, "If Allah loves a person, He calls Gabriel saying: 'Allah loves so and so; O Gabriel, love him.' Gabriel would love him, and then Gabriel would make an announcement among the residents of the Heavens, 'Allah loves so-and-so, therefore, you should love him also.' So, all the residents of the Heavens would love him and then he is granted the pleasure of the people of the earth."

(Sahih al Bukhari)

My lovely sister, we can sometimes feel overwhelmed by our circumstances and feel like nothing is going right for us. This leads to doubts and depression. This is our reminder, that Allah is the best exposer of all of our affairs and He Knows All.

He ﷻ understands each of us more than we understand ourselves. He is our Creator, our Sustainer, the One who fashioned us the way we are. He Knows things about us that we do not know and Ultimately Allah Knows what is best for us and what is not.

When one door closes all we see is no way out, however Allah ﷻ creates openings for us in places we could never have imagined.

Have faith dear sister, we are looked after. Remember, Allah's plans are the best of plans. If we place our full trust in Him, as we should, and rely solely on Him, we have nothing to worry about. Pray and turn to Allah in your times of need.

This applies to every aspect of our lives, from financial

situations, to emotional situations. From Deen related issues to Dunya related issues. Allah Knows what is best for us. It is up to us to accept that wholeheartedly.

Allah ﷻ reminds us in the Holy Qur'an; Surah al Baqarah verse 216:

"But perhaps you hate a thing and it is good for you; and perhaps you love a thing and it is bad for you. And Allah Knows, while you know not."

How many times have we really wanted something, and for some reason or another, we have been unable to attain it. This has led to emotional breakdowns, depression and sadness, which can sometimes last for a very long time. Later on, we realise how much of a blessing it was and how better off we are for not having that thing we wanted so badly.

At the time, we think it is the end of the world, or we treat it as such, but afterwards we thank Allah for turning us away from that affair. Alhamdulilah, Allah ﷻ saves us and closes one door for us only to open a better one to guide us through. Have faith. We rush into things and think it is the best thing for us, but in the long run, it may not be. When you ask Allah to guide you and leave it to His Majesty and Perfect Guidance, then you will find success waiting for you at every turn.

This complete and utter reliance upon Allah is called Tawakkul.

The importance of Tawakkul

Allah ﷻ says in the Holy Qur'an:

"And whoever fears Allah- He will make for him a way out. And will provide for him from where he does

not expect. And whoever relies upon Allah - then He is sufficient for him. Indeed, Allah will accomplish His purpose. Allah has already set for everything a [decreed] extent."

(Surah At-Talaq, verses 2 and 3)

Placing your trust in Allah ﷻ, means to accept the good and the bad that crosses our path and to have faith that the outcome of both will ultimately be good for us. For a believer, this is a requirement not an option. We submit to the will of Allah and trust that His decision for us is without a shadow of doubt, the best decision for us. We depend on Him and we rely upon Him Alone, ﷻ.

Furthermore, relying upon Allah ﷻ, does not mean that we cross our hands and legs and wait for blessings to pour down upon us without putting in the work for it. We can not expect Allah to send down our provision, food, and take care of our affairs whilst we sit around doing nothing. Yes we place our trust and reliance in our Rabb (Lord/Sustainer), but He has also blessed us with limbs and intellect to work towards what we wish to gain. We do what we can and leave the rest to Allah ﷻ. If we try our best and receive what we wished to gain, Alhamdulilah! If we try our best but do not gain it, Alhamdulilah! We praise Allah ﷻ in every circumstance and understand that there must be reasons behind not being granted that particular thing we worked for. This is trusting His plan. For there is only benefit in what He has decreed for us.

Anas ibn Malik reported:

A man said, "O Messenger of Allah, should I tie my camel and trust in Allah, or should I leave her untied and trust in Allah?" The Prophet ﷺ said, "Tie her and trust in Allah."

(Sunan al-Tirmidhi)

Life is difficult to bear on our own. Trusting Allah helps relieve us of worry and the weight of suffering. How wonderful are those moments when we turn to Him, and pour our heart out to Him. Knowing He alone Hears and understands the language of our heart, even when our lips are silent. May Allah ﷺ grant ease to us all and allow us to find comfort and peace in tawakkul and prayer.

The Story of Qadi Al-Maristan and the fruits of his tawakkal

A most beautiful example that comes to mind, and one of my most favourite stories to turn back to on the topic of Tawakkal, is the story of a person named Qadi al-Maristan which I have summarised below.

"Once Qadi was very hungry and could not find anything to eat. While looking for some food in the streets of Makkah where he lived, he found a pouch containing a beautiful necklace and he took it home. He had gone through a difficult time to the utmost ease, but his faith in Allah ﷺ (Tawakkul) did not waver a bit in his heart. As such, he kept the necklace and once again left to look for some food. From a far off place, he heard a person shouting in order to be heard amongst the throngs of people in the streets. "I have lost a necklace and I have 500 dinars in reward for whoever brings the necklace back to me".

On hearing this, Qadi rushed back home and returned the necklace to the old man.

On taking his necklace back, the old man offered the reward money of 500 dinar to Qadi. As he was about to take the money,

Qadi hesitated and thought to himself that the necklace hadn't been his in the first place so he didn't deserve to take money for returning it, and so he refused the reward.

The old man persisted and tried to convince him to take the reward but Qadi, although he was in desperate need of provision, kept his trust in Allah ﷻ and didn't accept it. The man left him and went about on his way.

A few years later, Qadi left Makkah with a group of people and took to the ocean, in the hope that he could find food and lodging elsewhere, but the ship he was sailing on sank on the way.

All the wealth and everyone aboard were flung into the dark seas and drowned. Qadi got hold of a small raft and it eventually guided him to an occupied island.

On landing there, he immediately rushed to a nearby mosque to thank Allah for saving him, but he found nobody there. He began reciting the Holy Qur'an and the sound of his recitation attracted people towards the mosque.

The people of the island offered him the position to teach them how to read and recite the Holy Qur'an. He accepted and was overwhelmed with gifts and food in payment. After some time living amongst them contently, he was offered the proposal of marrying a recently orphaned girl of a very rich man.

After a lot of insistence from the people of the island, he accepted and married her. Upon seeing the girl, who was now his wife, he happened to see the same necklace he had returned to the old man in Makkah years ago, hanging around her neck.

He was astonished and relayed the story of this necklace to the people. The people of the island were stunned and told Qadi, that the old man he had met in Makkah was the father of this orphaned girl and he used to pray, "O Allah, unite the man who returned my necklace with my daughter in marriage, as I have not seen any Muslim as good as him on the face of earth."

SubhanAllah! There are many beautiful lessons we can take from this story.

Qadi al-Maristan, although he had been in a very troubled time in his life and was desperately in need of food, he placed his entire trust in Allah ﷻ, and in reward Allah ﷻ changed his life around. Bear in mind, he went through a lot of hardship in the process and lost everything he had, and his hardships lasted many years. However, this was all a part of Allah's plan for him and Qadi never lost sight of that and his reliance upon Allah ﷻ stayed firm and unwavering. Allah ﷻ placed so many tests in his life, but they were all there so that he could reach the destination Allah ﷻ had planned for him. After which he lived a life of respect, ease and comfort.

Then pay attention to how this old man, who was so impressed by this young man's character and honesty, returned to the island he lived on, miles away from Makkah. He made what would seem to us to be an impossible dua, as he did not even know Qadi's name and there was such a distance between them. A whole sea between them.

Yet he prayed to Allah ﷻ, for is daughter to marry Qadi. This is just amazing. He had the firm trust that Allah ﷻ Hears every sincere call and so he prayed for the seemingly impossible.

In response, Allah ﷻ caused the idea of travelling to enter Qadi's mind, and then caused the ship he was sailing on to sink, just so that the little raft of wood would carry him to the remote island and in turn would lead him to marry the old man's daughter. SubhanAllah! Allah ﷻ truly makes the impossible possible and is the Best Disposer of all affairs.

Place your trust in Him! Solidify that trust and soothe your heart and mind with the Knowledge that if anyone is to answer your call it is Allah ﷻ alone.

Narrated by Abu Huraira: The Prophet ﷺ said, "Allah says:

"I am just as My slave thinks I am, (i.e. I am able to do for him what he thinks I can do for him) and I am with him if He remembers Me. If he remembers Me in himself, I too, remember him in Myself; and if he remembers Me in a group of people, I remember him in a group that is better than they; and if he comes one span nearer to Me, I go one cubit nearer to him; and if he comes one cubit nearer to Me, I go a distance of two outstretched arms nearer to him; and if he comes to Me walking, I go to him running.

(Sahih al Bukhari)

Allah ﷻ will always answer our call, whether that is by granting what we asked for or granting us better than that. We must have firm belief and conviction in our trust in Him and in doing so we will find only goodness in our life ahead. Ultimately Allah guides us to a path that is meant for us and fills the sincere heart with patience and hope. "When we get what we want- that is Allah's direction. When we do not- that is Allah's protection."

As believers we are strong and positive minded, and hold the belief that the Help of Allah is indeed near.

Al-Hasan al-Basri (may Allah have mercy on him) said:

"Do not resent the calamities that come and the disasters that occur, for perhaps in something that you dislike will be your salvation, and perhaps in something that you prefer will be your doom."

Al-Fadl ibn Sahl said:

"There is a blessing in calamity that the wise man should not ignore, for it erases sins, gives one the opportunity to attain the reward for patience, dispels negligence, reminds one of blessings at the time of health, calls one to repent and encourages one to give charity.

Remember my dear sister; Allah loves us.

More than our mothers love us. More than we think we love ourselves. More than anyone we hold dear loves us.

His Love is All Encompassing. He is The Most Compassionate, The Most Merciful. We need to seek out methods to attain His love, because His love guarantees success, safety and abundant rewards.

Let us make the intention right now, to work towards earning the Love of our Creator, to be consistent in our deeds and patient upon all that befalls us. Let us avoid all actions that could cause the anger of Allah, and rush towards deeds that are pleasing to him. May Allah allow us to remember and glorify Him often.

Abu Huraira reported that the Prophet Muhammad said that Allah, the Exalted and Glorious said:

"I am near to the thought of My servant as he thinks about Me, and I am with him as he remembers Me. And if he remembers Me in his heart, I also remember him in My heart, and if he remembers Me in assembly I remember him in assembly, better than his (remembrance), and if he draws near Me by the span of a palm, I draw near him by the cubit, and if he draws near me by the cubit I draw near him by the space

(covered by) two hands. And if he walks towards Me, I rush towards him."

[Sahih Muslim]

"When Allah tests you,

It is never to destroy you.

When He removes something in your possession,

It is in order to empty your hands, for an even greater gift!"

"A gem can not be polished without friction,   Nor a man perfected without trials."

CHAPTER 6

Bury your soul in supplication

The ability to supplicate directly to our Creator, is one of the greatest blessings that Allah has granted us. In it is peace, relief from distress and anxiety and a healing for the heavy heart.

A few sisters have told me they find it hard to think of the right words to make du'a with and so I shall include some supplications that can be found in the sunnah which we can use as guidelines. I pray they provide you with ideas on what you can ask for and they are available for you to pick up and use whenever need may be.

We all go through life needing solace and comfort and who is better to gain that comfort from than The One who Created us. He who Knows our inner most feelings without a word needing to escape our lips. He who understands our soul more than we understand it ourself; who loves us despite all of our weaknesses and errors.

Allah ﷻ has created us beautifully and we are given bodies that are perfect for child bearing and nurturing and we each have been blessed with a womb in which our children are held safely and in which they grow. This is one of the ways in which we surpass men and have been granted the huge responsibility of caring for our young.

The word for womb in arabic; "Rahim" is derived from the word Ar-Rahmaan (a name and attribute of Allah), meaning they're both from the same root word. i.e. Mercy. That is why mothers are full of mercy, because the womb is a place of mercy.

You may be wondering why I am mentioning the womb in a topic to do with supplications? Well, every month during our menstrual cycle we can not touch the Holy Qur'an or pray and fast as we would when we are in a state of purity. Sometimes this can cause our routine to break up and it affects a lot of sisters in their consistency in worship.

In that time however, we should increase in our supplications as making du'a is a very recommended necessary act of worship and we can make du'a in whatever state we are in. Many of us tend to be in an emotional state in those days and what better time to turn our soul towards Allah. When we are feeling down, in pain and upset because of hormonal imbalance, we should use that time to the best of our advantage, as we are more in tune with our emotional side.

This makes it easier for tears to flow and helps us connect with Allah in our most vulnerable moments.

Dear sister, during your period, sit on the prayer mat at every prayer time and do your adhkaar and make du'a in the time it would normally take for you to pray. This way bi idhnillah (with the permission of Allah ﷻ), you will keep up with the routine of stopping your worldly matters and turning towards Allah at the allotted prayer times; you will gain rewards for the adhkaar and du'as you make and you won't waste them days neglecting your remembrance of Allah ﷻ.

Pregnant sisters are especially encouraged to increase in their adhkaar and supplications, and to call upon Allah often throughout their pregnancy and labour.

Babies are said to recognise certain sounds from their time in the womb, and so increasing in reading the Holy Qur'an and calling upon Allah whilst pregnant is highly encouraged to bring about recognition.

Reciting "Ya Lateef" day and night and other of Allah's Virtuous Names, helps bring about ease and spiritual comfort during pregnancy.

Du'a is the weapon of the believer and the ability to talk to Allah ﷻ directly and is one of the greatest gifts and blessings bestowed upon us. It is such an important part of our faith and is the essence of worship, as The Messenger of Allah ﷺ said;

"The supplication is the essence of worship."

(Jami'-At-Tirmidhi)

In another hadith recorded in Sunan Abi Dawood, and narrated by Nu'man ibn Bashir, The Prophet ﷺ said:

Supplication (du'a) is itself worship.

(He then recited:) "And your Lord said: Call on Me, I will answer you" (xI.60).

It is our secret conversation with Our Creator, in which we can pour all our heart's hidden requests, desires, pains and worries; knowing that As-Sami' is Listening to our pleas, Al-Baseer is Watching over us.

Allah ﷺ says in the Holy Qur'an;

"And when My servants ask you, [O Muhammad], concerning Me - indeed I am near. I respond to the invocation of the supplicant when he calls upon Me. So let them respond to Me [by obedience] and believe in Me that they may be [rightly] guided."

(Surah al Baqarah, verse 186)

Du'a is submission to Allah ﷺ and demonstrates our dire need for His Help and Mercy. We accept He alone has the power to change our affairs and to accept our supplications.

We are encouraged to make du'a and supplicate often, in times of difficulty and in times of ease, for our own needs and for the needs of others. It is highly recommended to pray for others as we pray for ourselves as Islam encourages the community system and the concept of loving for your brother what you love for yourself.

Especially in the troubled times that we live in today; all over the world our brothers and sisters are being killed, tortured, bombed, and they are losing everything. It is so important that we pray for them.

When we pray for others, the angels supplicate in our favour too. So really we are gaining prayers for ourself.

Abu-Darda' reported: The Messenger of Allah ﷺ said,

"The supplication of a Muslim for his (Muslim) brother in his absence will certainly be answered. Every-time he makes a supplication for good for his brother, the angel appointed for this particular task says: 'Ameen! May it be for you, too'."

(Sahih Muslim)

In another similar hadith it has been recorded:

Abu Al-Darda' said:

I heard the Messenger of Allah say: When a Muslim supplicates for his absent brother the angels say: Amin, and may you receive the like.

(Sunan Abi Dawud)

Our parents, grandparents and family members have rights over us and from those rights is that we should pray for them whilst they are alive and after their passing. They are most deserving of our kindness and most deserving of our prayers.

Abu Hurayra reported that the Messenger of Allah ﷺ said,

"When a person dies, all action is cut off for him with the exception of three things:

Sadaqa which continues, Knowledge which benefits, or a righteous child who makes supplication for him."

(Al Adab Al-Mufrad)

Allah ﷻ always listens to and answers our prayers. Sometimes the answer may not be straight away or exactly in the way we expect. However, if we're patient we will surely see them answered and the outcome will always be better than what we asked for.

It was narrated from Abu Hurairah that: The Messenger of Allah ﷺ said:

"It is necessary that you do not become hasty." It was said: "What does being hasty mean, O Messenger of Allah?" He said: "When one says: 'I supplicated to Allah but Allah did not answer me.

(Sunan ibn Majah)

It is very important to supplicate and wait for results with sabr (patience). Allah ﷻ will answer When He likes and when it is better for us.

Abu Hurairah reported:

The Messenger of Allah said; The supplication of every one of you will be granted if he does not get impatient and say (for example): 'I supplicated to my Rubb but my prayer has not been granted'."

The narration of Muslim is: "The supplication of a slave continues to be granted as long as he does not supplicate for a sinful thing or for something that would cut off the ties of kinship and he does not grow impatient." It was said: "O Messenger of Allah! What does growing impatient mean?" He (ﷺ) said, "It is one's saying: 'I supplicated again and again but I do not think that my prayer will be answered.' Then he becomes frustrated (in such circumstances) and gives up supplication altogether."

(Riyadh as Saliheen)

Sunnah method and etiquettes of supplication

Islam is so beautiful. We have been taught exactly how to worship Allah in ways that are pleasing to Him. Whether that is how to pray, how to fast or how to make wudhu. Everything has been explained in detail making it an easy manual for us to follow.

Du'a also has certain methods and etiquettes which we must respect and adhere to if we want our supplications to bear fruit. Indeed Allah ﷻ does not turn away the empty hands of His slaves that are raised in front of Him, but He fills them with blessings and the reward of acceptance.

There are a few methods we have been taught on how to bring more substance and purpose to our du'as, and some situations in which our supplications will be accepted.

1. Start off by praising Allah ﷻ and sending salutations upon the Messenger of Allah ﷺ.

Fadalah bin Ubaid said:

"The Messenger of Allah ﷺ heard a man supplicating during the prayer without glorifying Allah ﷻ nor sending salah upon the Prophet ﷺ. The Messenger of Allah ﷺ said: 'You are in a hurry, O worshipper.' Then he taught them (the correct way). He heard a man praying; he glorified and praised Allah ﷻ and sent salah upon the Prophet ﷺ.

The Messenger of Allah ﷺ said:

'Supplicate, you will be answered; ask, you will be given.'"

(Sunan An-Nasa'i)

2.   Be firm in your supplication. Know what you are asking and ask with complete belief that Allah can grant it to you and will accept your du'as.

Anas reported Allah's Messenger ﷺ as saying:

When one of you makes supplication, he should supplicate with a will and should not say: O Allah, confer upon me if Thou likest, for there is none to coerce Allah.

(Sahih Muslim)

We are in need of Allah's Forgiveness and Mercy, and using the words "If You like" or "if You want", show an attitude of not caring if He grants us what we want or not. It is our job to ask clearly for what we wish for and to beg Him to grant it to us, for indeed, He is Most Capable of accepting our prayers.

Abu Hurairah reported the Messenger of Allah ﷺ as

saying:

"One of you should not say (in his supplication): O Allah, forgive me if You please, show mercy to me if You please.' Rather, be firm in your asking, for no one can force Him."

(Sunan Abi Dawud)

3. Praise Allah ﷻ and invoke Him using His beautiful Names and Attributes, befitting to that which you are asking Him.

Allah ﷻ says in The Holy Qur'an

And to Allah ﷻ belong the best names, so invoke Him by them. And leave [the company of] those who practice deviation concerning His names. They will be recompensed for what they have been doing.

(Surah Al-A'raf, verse 180)

In another verse it says,

Say, "Call upon Allah or call upon the Most Merciful. Whichever [name] you call - to Him belong the best names." And do not recite [too] loudly in your prayer or [too] quietly but seek between that an [intermediate] way.

(Surah Al-Israa, verse 110)

It is recorded in a hadith that, Abu Hurairah narrated:

When a matter would worry the Prophet ﷺ he would raise his head up toward the sky and say: "Glory is to

Allah, the Magnificent (Subhān Allāhil-'Azīm)." And when he would strive in supplication; he would say: "O the Living, O Sustainer (Yā Hayyu yā Qayyūm)

(Jami' at-Tirmidhi)

Narrated by Anas ibn Malik:

I was sitting with the Messenger of Allah ﷺ *and a man was offering prayer. He then made the supplication: O Allah, I ask Thee by virtue of the fact that praise is due to Thee, there is no deity but Thou, Who show-est favour and beneficence, the Originator of the Heavens and the earth, O Lord of Majesty and Splendour, O Living One, O Eternal One. The Prophet* ﷺ *then said: He has supplicated to Allah using His Greatest Name, when supplicated by this name, He answers, and when asked by this name He gives.*

(Sunan Abi Dawud)

4. Turn to face the Qiblah and have complete focus whilst supplicating. This is the sunnah of The Messenger of Allah ﷺ and is the best direction in which to face and make du'a.

Narrated by 'Ali bin Abi Talib:

"We departed with the Messenger of Allah ﷺ *until he was at Harrah As-Suqya which belonged to Sa'd bin Abi Waqqas. So the Messenger of Allah said: 'Bring me water for Wudhu.' So he performed Wudhu, then he faced the Qiblah and said: 'O Allah! Indeed Ibrahim was Your servant and Your Khalil, and he supplicated for blessings for the people of Makkah. And I am Your*

servant and Messenger, and I supplicate for the people of Al-Madinah; that You bless them in their Mudd and their Sa' like You blessed the people of Makkah, for each blessing let there be two blessings."

(Jami' At-Tirmidhi)

5. Ask frequently and do not lose hope. Don't restrict yourself when making du'a and have firm faith that your du'a will be accepted. Don't make a du'a once or twice and then give up thinking you haven't seen any results. Allah Loves consistency in good deeds.

6. Make plenty of du'a in prostration. With your forehead on the ground you are in the most humble position in front of your Lord.

Abu Hurairah reported: The Messenger of Allah ﷺ said,

"A slave becomes nearest to his Rubb when he is in prostration. So increase supplications in prostrations."

(Sahih Muslim)

Ibn 'Abbas reported: The Messenger of Allah ﷺ said:

"Glorify your Lord in Ruku' (bowing posture) and exert yourself in supplication in prostration. Thus your supplications are liable to be accepted."

(Sahih Muslim, Riyadh as-Saaliheen)

7. Make your supplications comprehensive yet precise. Talk to Allah ﷻ about everything that bothers your heart, even if you feel like it is a little insignificant thing. Your Lord Knows you best and it will make you feel better.

8. Have humility in the way you ask, remember who you are asking from and don't transgress your boundaries. Allah ﷻ Loves when His slaves beseech Him privately and with humility.

Allah ﷻ says in The Holy Qur'an,

Call upon your Lord in humility and privately; indeed, He does not like transgressors.

(Surah Al-A'raf verse 55)

9. If you run out of words or can't find the words to describe how you are feeling or how to ask Allah for something, don't shorten your du'a as a result, rather sit in silence asking Allah ﷻ to grant you all that is in your heart that you are unable to put in to words. Sometimes the words come to us when we sit and think so don't hurry in your du'a.

10. Raise your hands, with your palms facing upwards.

Ibn 'Abbas said:

Earnest supplication should be made like this: he raised his hand and made his palms in the direction of his face.

(Sunan Abi Dawud)

11. Increase in du'a in the times The Messenger of Allah ﷺ has taught us are the best times for supplications. Praying for your needs at these times are guaranteed to be accepted and are most recommended.

Anas radi Allahu anhu reported: The Messenger of Allah ﷺ said:

"The supplication made between the Adhan and the Iqamah is never rejected."

(Abu Dawud and At-Tirmidhi)

Abu Umamah radi Allahu anhu reported: The Messenger of Allah ﷺ was asked:

"At what time does the supplication find the greatest response?" He ﷺ replied, "A supplication made during the middle of the last part of the night and after the conclusion of the obligatory prayers."

(At-Tirmidhi)

It was narrated from 'Abdullah bin 'Amr bin 'As that the Messenger of Allah ﷺ said:

"When the fasting person breaks his fast, his supplication is not turned back."

(Sunan Ibn Majah)

And worship Allah and increase in prayer in the third part of the night.

Abu Huraira reported Allah's Messenger ﷺ as saying:

Allah descends every night to the lowest heaven when one-third of the first part of the night is over and says: I am the Lord; I am the Lord: who is there to supplicate to Me so that I answer him? Who is there to beg of Me so that I grant him? Who is there to beg forgiveness from Me so that I forgive him? He ﷺ continues like this till the day breaks.

12. Supplicate when travelling. The traveller's supplications are never returned without being accepted.

Abu Hurairah reported: The Messenger of Allah said,

"Three supplications are answered without doubt. The supplication of the oppressed, the supplication of the traveller, and the supplication of the parent for his son."

(At-Tirmidhi and Abu Dawud)

13. Request supplications from the sick when you visit them. This will increase the likelihood of your du'a being accepted, as Allah's Mercy rains down upon the ill and needy.

Umar ibn al Khattab radi Allahu anhu said:

The Prophet ﷺ said to me; "When you enter upon one who is sick, tell him to pray for you, for his supplication is like the supplication of the angels."

(Sunan Ibn Majah)

14. Supplicate abundantly when it rains. When rain falls it is a time of great bounty and Mercy from Allah, and it is a time that is considered good to supplicate in if you wish for your du'a to be accepted.

The Prophet ﷺ said:

"Two supplications are not rejected: du'a at the time of the call to prayer and du'a at the time of rain.

(Narrated by al-Haakim in al-Mustadrak and at-

15. End your du'a by sending blessings upon The Messenger of Allah ﷺ.

The Prophet ﷺ said:

"Every du'a is kept back until you send blessings upon the Prophet ﷺ."

(Narrated by al-Tabaraani in al-Awsat)

I hope these tips help you structure your supplications and I pray Allah accepts them all from you and from us all.

Without a doubt, our beloved Prophet ﷺ is an example for us in every way. He is Allah's most beloved creation and whatever he asks from Allah ﷻ, Allah grants to him.

He has taught us how to make du'a and which du'as are best through his beautiful, perfect example. His whole life was spent in submission and prayer to Allah, which is why we can find supplications to make for everything we do in the sunnah.

His words are the best of words, his supplications are the best of supplications, his speech is the most beautiful of speech.

There are many supplications made by our beloved Prophet ﷺ which have been carefully recorded in ahadith and preserved for the ummah to use in their own supplications. These aid us in making clear, concise, and meaningful prayers and are supplications Allah ﷻ loves, as the Messenger of Allah ﷺ never spoke anything except that which came from Allah ﷻ.

Dear sister, I am including 30 ahadith which mention the wording of the supplications made by RasulAllah ﷺ.

If you ever run out of things to ask for, or want to include the beautiful supplications the Messenger of Allah ﷺ made to Allah, then I am sure these will be of use to you.

Few Gems from the Sunnah; Supplications of The Messenger of Allah ﷺ

I.

Narrated by Abu Hurairah radi Allahu anhu: The Messenger of Allah ﷺ used to say:

"O Allah, I seek refuge in Thee from four things: Knowledge which does not profit, a heart which is not submissive, a soul which has an insatiable appetite, and a supplication which is not heard."

(Sunan Abi Dawud)

2.

Qatada radi Allahu anhu asked Anas radi allahu anhu which Supplication Allah's Apostle ﷺ frequently made. He said: The supplication that he ﷺ made very frequently is this:

"O Allah, grant us the good in this world and the good in the Hereafter and save us from the torment of Hell-Fire." He (Qatada) said that whenever Anas had to supplicate he made this very supplication, and whenever he intended to make another supplication he included this very supplication in that.

(Sahih Muslim)

3.

Abu Hurairah radi Allahu anhu said: "The Messenger of Allah ﷺ used to say in his supplication:

'Allahumma inni a'udhu bika minash-shiqaqi wan-nifaqi, wa suw'il-akhlaq

(O Allah, I seek refuge with You from opposing the truth, hypocrisy and bad manners.)'"

(Sunan An-Nasa'I)

4.

It was narrated that Abu Hurairah said: "The Messenger of Allah ﷺ said:

'There is no supplication that a person can say that is better than: Allahumma inni as'aluka al-mu'afah fid-dunya wal-akhirah (O Allah, I ask You for Al-Mu'afah in this world and in the Hereafter).'"

(Sunan Ibn Majah)

5.

Ibrahim bin Muhammad bin Sa`d narrated from his father, from Sa`d that the Messenger of Allah ﷺ said:

"The supplication of Dhun-Nun (Prophet Yunus) when he supplicated, while in the belly of the whale was:

'There is none worthy of worship except You, Glory to

You, Indeed, I have been of the transgressors. (Lā ilāha illā anta subhānaka innī kuntu minaz-zālimīn)' So indeed, no Muslim man supplicates with it for anything, ever, except Allah responds to him."

(jami' At-Tirmidhi)

6.

Abdullah reported that Allah's Messenger ﷺ used to supplicate (in these words):

" O Allah. I beg of Thee the right guidance, safeguard against evils, chastity and freedom from want."

(Sahih Muslim)

7.

Mu'adh b. Jabal reported that the Messenger of Allah ﷺ caught his hand and said:

By Allah, I love you, Mu'adh. I give some instruction to you. Never leave to recite this supplication after every (prescribed) prayer: "O Allah, help me in remembering You, in giving You thanks, and worshipping You well."

Mu'adh willed this supplication to the narrator al-Sunabihi and al-Sunabihi to 'Abu Abd al-Rahman.

(Sunan Abi Dawud)

8.

'Abd Allah b. 'Umar radi Allahu anhuma said that one of the supplications of the Messenger of Allah ﷺ was:

"O Allah, I seek refuge in You that Your blessings are lifted, and Your protection (of me) is changed, and in the suddenness of Your punishment, and from all Your anger.

(Sunan Abi Dawud)

9.

Farwa' b. Naufal Ashja'i reported:

I asked: 'A'isha, in what words did Allah's Messenger supplicate to Allah? She said that he used to utter:" I seek refuge in Thee from the evil of what I did and from the evil of what I did not."

(Sahih Muslim)

10.

Abdullah b. Umar reported that Allah's Messenger ﷺ supplicated in these words:

" O Allah, I seek refuge in Thee from the withdrawal of Thine blessing and the change of Thine protection (from me) and from the sudden wrath of Thine, and from every displeasure of Thine."

(Sahih Muslim)

11.

Abdur-Rahman ibn Abu Bakrah said that he told his father:

O my father! I hear you supplicating every morning: "O Allah! Grant me health in my body. O Allah! Grant me good hearing. O Allah! Grant me good eyesight. There is no God but Thou." You repeat them three times in the morning and three times in the evening.

His father said: I heard the Messenger of Allah ﷺ using these words as a supplication and I like to follow his practice.

The transmitter, Abbas, said in his version: And you say: "O Allah! I seek refuge in Thee from infidelity and poverty. O Allah! I seek refuge in Thee from punishment in the grave. There is no god but Thee".

The Messenger of Allah ﷺ said: The supplications to be used by one who is distressed are: "O Allah! Thy mercy is what I hope for. Do not abandon me to myself for an instant, but put all my affairs in good order for me. There is no God but Thou." Some transmitters added more than others.

(Sunan Abi Dawud)

12.

A man came to the Prophet ﷺ and said:

"O Messenger of Allah, which supplication is the best?" He ﷺ said: "Ask Your Lord For Al-`Āfiyah and Al-Mu`āfāh in this world and in the Hereafter."

Then he came to him on the second day and said: "O Messenger of Allah, which supplication is the best?" So he ﷺ said to him similar to that. Then he came to him on the third day, so he ﷺ said to him similar to that. He ﷺ said: "So when you have been given Al-ʿĀfiyah in this world, and you have been given it in the Hereafter, then you have succeeded."

(Jami' At-Tirmidhi)

13.

"Allāhumma innā nas'aluka min khairi mā sa'alaka minhu nabiyyuka Muhammad, sallallāhu ʿalaihi wa sallam, wa naʿūdhu bika min sharri mastaʿādha minhu nabiyyuka Muhammad, sallallāhu ʿalaihi wa sallam, wa antal-mustaʿānu wa ʿalaikal-balāgh, wa lā hawla wa lā quwwata illā billāh"

(O Allah, we ask You from the good of what Your Prophet Muhammad ﷺ asked You for, and we seek refuge in You from the evil of that which Your Prophet Muhammad ﷺ sought refuge in You from, and You are the one from Whom aid is sought, and it is for You to fulfil, and there is no might or power except by Allah)

(Jami' At-Tirmidhi)

14.

ʿAbdullah bin ʿAmr narrated from Abu Bakr As-Siddiq radi Allahu anhu that he said:

"O Messenger of Allah, teach me a supplication that I

may supplicate with in my Salat." The Prophet ﷺ *said:*
"Say:

'O Allah, I have wronged myself much, and none forgives
sins except You. So forgive me with forgiveness from You,
and have mercy upon me, indeed, You are the Forgiving,
the Merciful.*

(Jami' At- Tirmidhi)

15.

'Aishah (May Allah be pleased with her) reported:

Prior to his demise, the Messenger of Allah ﷺ *used to
supplicate frequently: Subhan Allahi wa bihamdihi;
Astaghfirullaha wa atubu ilaihi (Allah is free from
imperfection, and I begin with praising Him. I beg
forgiveness from Allah and I turn to Him in repentance."*

(Sahih al-Bukhari and Muslim)

16.

It was narrated that Anas bin Malik said:

"The Messenger of Allah ﷺ *had supplications that he
never omitted to recite. He used to say: 'Allahumma
inni a'udhu bika minal-hammi, wal-hazani, wal-'ajzi,
wal-kasali, wal-bukhli, wal-jubni, wa ghalabatar-
rijal (O Allah, I seek refuge with You from worry, grief,
incapacity, laziness, miserliness, cowardice and being
overpowered by men."*

17.

'Abd Allah b. 'Abbas said:

The Messenger of Allah ﷺ *used to teach us this supplication as he taught us the surah from the Qur'an. He would say: O Allah! I seek refuge in You from the punishment of Hell and I seek refuge in You from the punishment of the grave, and I seek refuge from You from the trails of Al-Masihid-Dajjal, and I seek refuge in You from the trials of life and death.*

(Sunan Abi Dawud)

18.

Abu Malik reported on the authority of his father that when a person embraced Islam, Allah's Messenger ﷺ used to teach them how to observe prayer and then commanded them to supplicate in these words:

" O Allah, grant me pardon, have mercy upon me, direct me to the path of righteousness, grant me protection and provide me sustenance."

(Sahih Muslim)

19.

Abu Huraira reported that Allah's Messenger ﷺ used to supplicate (in these words):

" O Allah, set right for me my religion which is the safeguard of my affairs. And set right for me the affairs of my world wherein is my living. And set right for me my Hereafter on which depends my after-life. And make the life for me (a source) of abundance for every good and make my death a source of comfort for me protecting me against every evil."

(Sahih Muslim)

20.

The Prophet ﷺ said, "The best supplication for seeking forgiveness (Syed-ul- Istighfar) is to say:

'Allahumma Anta Rabbi, la ilaha illa Anta, khalaqtani wa ana 'abduka, wa ana 'ala 'ahdika wa wa'dika mastata'tu, a'udhu bika min sharri ma sana'tu, abu'u laka bini'matika 'alayya, wa abu'u bidhanbi faghfir li, fa innahu la yaghfirudh-dhunuba illa Anta.

(O Allah! You are my Rubb. There is no true god except You. You have created me, and I am Your slave, and I hold to Your Covenant as far as I can. I seek refuge in You from the evil of what I have done. I acknowledge the favours that You have bestowed upon me, and I confess my sins. Pardon me, for none but You has the power to pardon).' He who supplicates in these terms during the day with firm belief in it and dies on the same day (before the evening), he will be one of the dwellers of Jannah; and if anyone supplicates in these terms during the night with firm belief in it and dies before the

morning, he will be one of the dwellers of Jannah."

(Sahih Al Bukhari)

21.

The Messenger of Allah ﷺ said:

"Place light in my heart, light in my tongue, light in my hearing, light in my sight, light above me, light below me, light on my right, light on my left, light in front of me, light behind me, place light in my soul and make light abundant for me."

(Sahih Muslim)

22.

Narrated by Abu Huraira: The Messenger of Allah ﷺ used to supplicate by saying: "O Allah, I seek refuge in Thee from divisiveness, hypocrisy, and evil character."

(Sunan Abi Dawud)

23.

The Messenger of Allah ﷺ used to say when bowing and prostrating: "SubhanakAllahuma, Rabbana wa bihamdik. Allahumma-ghfirli (Glory be to You O Allah, Our Lord, and praise. O Allah, forgive me," following the command of the Qur'an.

(Sunan An-Nisa'i)

24.

Ibn Umar said, "The Messenger of Allah ﷺ did not omit saying the following words in the morning and evening:

'O Allah, I sak you for well-being in this world and the Next. O Allah, I ask you for forgiveness and well-being in my deen and in this world and in my family and my property. O Allah, veil my faults and calm my fears. O Allah, give me protection in front of me and behind me, on my right and my left and above me. I seek refuge by Your Might from being overwhelmed from under me."

(Al-Adab Al-Mufrad)

25.

Anas bin Malik narrated The Prophet ﷺ would say:

"O Allah, I seek refuge in You from a prayer that is of no benefit."

(Sunan Abi Dawud)

26.

A'isha radi Allaha anha said: *"I heard the Messenger of Allah ﷺ saying at his death: 'O Allah, forgive me have mercy on me, and join me with the Highest Company (Allahummaghfirli warhamni wa alhiqni bir-rafiqil a'la)."*

(Jami' At-Tirmidhi)

27.

Anas radi Allahu anhu reported that the Messenger of Allah used to supplicate in these words:

"Our Lord, grant us the good in this world and the good in the Hereafter and save us from the torment of Hell-fire."

(Sahih Muslim)

28.

A'isha reported that Allah's Messenger used to make these supplications:

"O Allah, I seek refuge in Thee from Hell-fire and from the torment of Hell-fire; and from the trial of the grave and torment of the grave; and from the evil of the trial of affluence and from the evil of the trial of poverty and I seek refuge in Thee from the evil of the turmoil of the Dajjal. O Allah, wash away my sins with snow and hail water, purify my heart from the sins as is purified the white garment from the dirt, and keep away at a distance the sins from me as yawns the distance between the East and the West; O Allah, I seek refuge in Thee from sloth, from senility, from sin and from debt."

(Sahih Muslim)

29.

Al Bara' bin 'Azib reported that Allah's Messenger ﷺ said: When you go to bed, perform ablution as is done for prayer, then lie down on the right side and recite:

"O Allah, I turn my face towards Thee and entrust my affair to Thee. I retreat unto Thee for protection with hope in Thee and fear if Thee. There is no resort and no deliverer (from hardship) but Thou only. I affirm my faith in Thine books which Thou revealed and in Thine Apostles whom Thou sent." Make this as the last word of yours (when you go to sleep) and in case you die during the night, you would die upon Fitra (Islam).

(Sahih Muslim)

30.

Abu Huraira radi Allahu anhu reported that Allah's Messenger ﷺ used to supplicate (in these words):

"O Allah, set right for me my religion which is the safeguard of my affairs. And set right for me the affairs of my world wherein is my living. And set right for me my Hereafter on which depends my after-life. And make the life for me (a source) of abundance for every good and make my death a source of comfort for me protecting me against every evil."

(Sahih Muslim)

May Allah accept all of our supplications and raise us amongst the righteous on the Day of Judgement.

"When Allah inspires your tongue to ask,

Know that He wants to give."

&

"Your voice is heard by Allah, when you think no-one can hear you."

PART 4

PRACTICAL STEPS TOWARDS A PURER YOU

CHAPTER 7

Count The Blessings Allah Has Bestowed Upon You

Start your day in praise of Him and end it in praise of Him. Ponder upon all of the ways you have been blessed and think of the things in your life that make you happy. Things you have that others may not be fortunate enough to possess; whether that is having a roof over your head or a fridge full of food.

He has blessed you with sight and hearing, the ability to smell and touch and blessed you with Islam. All that you have is a blessing from Allah and a reason to be grateful and thank Him.

My dear sister, do not compare your situation to the situation of others, as each individual, each family, each household has troubles of their own.

Do not obsess over those with more than you, rather look at those who have less than you and thank Allah for the bounties you have that they would love to own.

The more we focus on things we don't have, the more we fall prey to our own greed. Negative thoughts bring nothing but unhappiness and a loss of satisfaction. It is the feeding ground to many ill thoughts and sicknesses of the heart, such as jealousy and anger.

However, if we focus more on all the things we do have we will have a more optimistic approach to life and it will bring us contentment and happiness. This will lead to a cleaner heart, making us happier for the success of others, and content with what we have. We should give thanks to Allah for all of the blessings we enjoy. The more we thank Him, the more He will grant us. The happier our thoughts, the more satisfied with our lives we will be.

"Gratitude lifts our eyes off the things we lack so we might see the blessings we possess."

-

Kindness Towards Others Is The Recipe For Inner Peace.

"I've been searching for ways to heal myself, and I've found that kindness is the best way."

Allah has blessed women with a naturally caring and kind heart. When you use this quality often, your whole aura becomes one of love and peace. This in turn affects your inner and outer self, making you much happier.

People will treat you how you treat them. If you treat them gently and with affection they will treat you the same. This will create a peaceful, enjoyable environment to live in and will work wonders for your heart.

Islam teaches us to be kind; kind to our parents, kind to our children, kind to our neighbours, to animals, to nature and to every human being regardless of age, status and faith.

Jabir reported that the Messenger of Allah ﷺ said,

"Every act of kindness is sadaqah. Part of kindness is that you offer your brother a cheerful face and you pour some of your bucket into his water vessel."

(Al-Adab Al-Mufrad)

When you have a good manner and kindly attitude you will have more peace of mind and are less likely to find yourself in an unhappy situation. Remember those closest to you are in more need of your kindness and love. They are the ones who should receive your joyful smile first.

It's quite remarkable how even the smallest show of kindness can have such a positive effect on a person.

The Henry Ford Livewell Health System states, "studies were conducted which show that smiling not only offers a mood boost but also helps our bodies release cortisol and endorphins that provide numerous health benefits, including:

- Reduced blood pressure.
- Increased endurance
- Reduced pain
- Reduced stress
- Strengthened immune system

Furthermore, studies show that people who smile appear more likeable, courteous and competent. Smilers tend to be more productive at work and make more money."

Abdullah ibn Harith reports, "I did not see anyone who smiled more than the Messenger of Allah ﷺ.

(Shama'il Muhammadiyah)

Having a good kindly attitude is an act of worship to Allah and an easy way to gain the love of those on Earth and in the Heavens.

"Love and kindness are never wasted. They always make a difference. They bless the one who receives them, and they bless you, the giver."

-

Be Productive & Organised.

Having some kind of structure to your day will help you make the most of your time. A productive woman has the potential to do much good as she uses her time efficiently. Keep yourself busy and stop yourself from becoming a victim of idleness. The busier your day, the less time you have to fall into depressing thoughts and stronger sense of achievement you will feel at the end.

Busy yourself in work and worship, and you will find yourself happier than you were before. An idle mind is the playground of the devil. He wants us to feel depressed and unhappy and a mind unoccupied with work or duty is his easiest victim.

There is no harm in having a rest, we all need rest to function properly, however don't let them rests lead to a prolonged period of laziness. How many times do we have a job to do but we procrastinate and spend the time we had planned working, in doing nothing at all. This is just delaying the inevitable and when you finally get around to working you'll realise how much more work has piled up on top of the original amount that needed doing. This makes a person feel overwhelmed and upset and makes them want to give up.

If we use our time wisely, we can tackle each job as it comes, and then we have no mental burden and can enjoy ourselves at the same time.

Laziness leads to depression and a build up of anxiety. However, in productivity you shall find happiness and joy.

The more free time we have the easier it is to fall into sins like back-biting which we fall prey to when we have too much time on our hands. If Shaytan can not make us sin, he will try to make us waste time instead. Valuable time that we could have spent in growing closer to Allah and in learning our Deen.

Every moment we live is precious and is time we wont get back. Make good use of your time and try to keep yourself busy in matters that will benefit your Dunya and your Aakhirah.

"Replace excuses with effort,

replace laziness with determination

And everything else will fall into place"

-

A Healthy Woman Is A Happy Woman

Good health is the spirit of happiness. You have been blessed with a beautiful able body and it is your duty to look after this gift from Allah. Eating healthy, exercising and drinking plenty of water is a must to look and feel well.

A believer lives their life in moderation and this applies to every part of their life. Eating moderately, enough but not too much is an important part of this practice. Over-eating leads to laziness, greed and health problems. Our Deen is so complete there are even lessons for us to learn from, regarding how to eat and how much to eat.

Narrated by Abu Huraira:

A man used to eat a lot, but when he embraced Islam he started eating less. That was mentioned to the Prophet ﷺ who then said. "A believer eats in one intestine (is satisfied with a little food) and a Kafir eats in seven intestines (eats much)."

(Sahih al-Bukhari)

My dear sister, Islam encourages a healthy, active lifestyle. Enjoy your food but do not eat in excess. You will be amazed at how good you will feel internally as well as externally when you practice eating just enough, and exercising often.

There are many kinds of physical activities you can do to keep fit, including swimming, running, walking and jogging. If you enjoy sports there are an endless list of options to have fun and lose calories at the same time. You don't even need to go out of the home.

Being active has many health benefits both mentally, spiritually and physically. It has proven to improve your mood and decrease feelings of depression, anxiety and stress. It can increase the production of endorphins which are known to help produce positive feelings.

It helps us discipline our mind and soul and increases our energy levels. This is especially good for a muslim, who can use that heightened energy for worship and standing longer in prayer.

Overall, staying active and eating less makes us happier and more productive.

Miqdam ibn Ma'd reported: the Messenger of Allah ﷺ said,

"The son of Adam cannot fill a vessel worse than his stomach, as it is enough for him to take a few bites to straighten his back.

If he can't do this, then he may fill it with a third of his food, a third of his drink and a third of air."

(Sunan At-Tirmidhi)

"Moderation. Small helpings. Sample a bit of everything. These are the secrets of happiness and good health."

-

Prioritise Worship & Strengthen Your Faith.

The most important step towards inner peace and contentment is making the effort to repair your connection with your Creator. This is the ingredient which will ultimately result in your peace of heart, mind and soul, and will guarantee you success in this life and in the Hereafter.

My dear sister, we are all searching for happiness and a purpose to our lives and worshipping Allah is our true purpose; the reason we have been created. This is what our heart craves for the most.

The stronger our connection to Allah ﷻ, the more content we are in every situation. The more comfort we find in worship, the more we feel complete and are filled with feelings of happiness.

"The purpose of life is to achieve real happiness by

Worshipping the One True God in everything that we

do."

A life without the remembrance and worship of Allah is a desolate, depressed life indeed. The sweetness of faith and prayer, water the dead heart and bring life to the soul, causing it to bloom.

True comfort is found only in obeying Allah and focusing on improving the quality of your worship. Whoever obeys Him and follows his commands and Loves to worship Him will find comfort and joy in being close to Him.

When your heart is heavy, burdened with sins and grief and you feel you have strayed from the straight path for too long, turn to Him. When you feel you have done too much wrong for too long, turn to Him. The doors of repentance are open and Allah is waiting for his servants to turn back to Him. He loves those who repent and satisfies their heart with tranquillity in return.

Narrated by Anas bin Malik: Allah's Messenger said,

"Allah is more pleased with the repentance of His slave than anyone of you is pleased with finding his camel which he had lost in the desert."

(Sahih al-Bukhari)

When you stand before your Lord with a heavy heart and mind, He lifts the burdens of guilt from you and places sakeenah in your heart.

This is the happiness and sweetness of faith only felt by repairing your connection with Allah.

He is waiting for You, and waiting to fill your heart and soul with relief and joy. Reconnect and Rejoice!

"And if Allah should touch you with adversity, there is no remover of it except Him; and if He intends for you good, then there is no repeller of His bounty. He causes it to reach whom He wills of His servants. And He is the Forgiving, the Merciful"

(Surah Yunus, verse 107)

"There are no sad endings for those who trust Allah."

-

With Love

My dear sister in Islam, I pray you found this book a light comforting read. I pray it serves as a reminder of your honoured position as a Muslim woman.

May Allah always keeps you in His protection.

Keep your head held high, don't let that crown slip from your head. May Allah allow us to walk amongst the righteous in the beautiful gardens of paradise and I pray He guides us towards deeds that are most pleasing to Him.

It is not easy being a Muslimah but always remember; our reward is with Our Creator, and this life will not last forever.

Let us keep our focus on our Life in the Hereafter and let us concentrate on excelling in our faith.

I pray Allah rewards you for every effort you make for His Sake.

May we become great women and may we raise great children, who work hard for the betterment of society and who pride themselves in their islamic identity.

I end with this continuous reminder in the Holy Qur'an,

Allah ﷻ says;

"Indeed, the Muslim men and Muslim women, the believing men and believing women, the obedient men and obedient women, the truthful men and truthful women, the patient men and patient women, the humble men and humble women, the charitable men and charitable women, the fasting men and fasting women, the men who guard their private parts and the women who do so, and the men who remember Allah often and the women who do so - for them Allah has prepared forgiveness and a great reward."

(Surah al-Ahzab, verse 35)

ACKNOWLEDGEMENTS

I would like to thank my mother, for believing in me and for encouraging me every step of the way. I could not have achieved much of what I have, if I did not have your continuous support and love.

Thank you, for being my role model and living embodiment of how a believing woman should conduct herself in all matters.

Thank you, to my sisters, who I have looked up to all my life, and without whom, my life would be most incomplete.

Thank you, to my teachers, who nurtured me and taught me the value of my Deen, brought me closer to My creator and helped me understand the purpose of life.

Thank you to KC, who designed my front cover beautifully and to the Leaf Publishing team for bringing this book to life.

And as always, I want to thank YOU, dear reader, for your time and I hope you enjoy this book, as much as I have enjoyed writing it.

Cover designed and illustrated by @kcartci
You can find her on Instagram and Twitter by the same name

Lightning Source UK Ltd.
Milton Keynes UK
UKHW041431230821
389329UK00003B/549